# THE KIDS'
# WINTER
## FUN BOOK

First edition for the United States, its territories and dependencies, and
Canada published in 2011 by Barron's Educational Series, Inc.

Copyright © 2011 Elwin Street Productions
Conceived and produced by Elwin Street Productions
144 Liverpool Road
London N1 1LA
United Kingdom
www.elwinstreet.com

All inquiries should be addressed to:
Barron's Educational Series, Inc.
250 Wireless Blvd.
Hauppauge, NY  11788
www.barronseduc.com

ISBN-13: 978-0-7641-4726-5

Library of Congress Control Number: 2011922075

The activities described in this book are to be carried out with parental
supervision at all times. Every effort has been made to ensure the safety of the
activities detailed. Neither the author nor the publishers shall be liable or
responsible for any harm or damage done allegedly arising from any
information or suggestion in this book.

Picture credits:
Corbis: p. 87; Dreamstime: pp. 47, 53, 70; Getty Images: pp. 15, 111;
iStock images: pp. 8, 23, 31, 32, 37, 38, 72, 86, 104, 107, 114, 125.

Illustrations by: David Eaton

Printed in China

9 8 7 6 5 4 3 2 1

# THE KIDS' WINTER FUN BOOK

## HOMESPUN ADVENTURES FOR FAMILY FUN

### CLAIRE GILLMAN
### & SAM MARTIN

BARRON'S

# CONTENTS

## INTRODUCTION

## 1 CRAFTING

Let your creativity run wild with these fantastic things to make and do.

## 2 OUTDOOR PLAY

Just because it's cold outside, you don't have to stay indoors. There are plenty of fun activities to keep you busy and warm.

## 3 INDOOR PLAY

Fun ideas you can get the whole family involved in.

## 4 FEASTING

Treat yourself during the winter months with these seasonal, festive and warming snacks.

## INDEX  128

# INTRODUCTION

Spring has its blossom and summer its sun, while fall is known for its colorful displays of turning leaves. But for rosy-cheeked fun with family and friends, it's hard to beat winter. When the thermometer dips and plump flakes of snow twirl idly through the air, it heralds the beginning of a season of delights, such as building snowmen and sledding down snow-capped hills. The home becomes a haven of warmth and companionship, with the welcoming aroma of comforting foods cooking in the kitchen and a fire crackling in the hearth. Add the merry chatter of friends and the chill of the season vanishes entirely—and you begin to realize that, in some ways, winter can be the most warming season of all.

To help you pack the most fun into the short days and long evenings of winter, this book contains a sleigh-load of activities to enjoy both in the home and outdoors. People have long gathered closely together for warmth and companionship during the winter months, so you will find many traditional indoor games to enjoy, ranging from absorbing storytelling activities to weird and wonderful science experiments that will amuse and entertain you for hours. Or, why not try your hand at something creative—make a leaf press with the fallen leaves, a snake draft stopper to keep out the cold, or design a board game for the long evenings spent inside.

If the sun is shining on freshly laid snow, however, you'll find even more to enjoy out of doors, such as making art with ice, building a snow fort, or even staging your own expedition. Then, after a whole day of playing, come inside and prepare a delicious snack or meal. Whether savory or sweet, you will find a suitable recipe within these pages,

Try all of the activities in *The Kids' Winter Fun Book* to discover just how enjoyable the coldest season can be. As the old saying goes, there's no such thing as bad weather, only unsuitable clothing—so wrap up warm, knot your best woollen scarf snugly around your neck, and enjoy all that winter has to offer. This book is every child's guide to fun all the way through the winter months.

## HOW TO USE THIS BOOK

Some of the winter activities in this book are more tricky or time-consuming than others, and you may want to make sure you have a group of family or friends gathered to give you a helping hand. Every activity is graded for difficulty and shows the amount of time that you will need to be able to complete it. So, whether you have just a few minutes to play indoors, or a whole day to spend outside, you'll never be stuck without anything to do.

One snowflake symbol indicates a project or activity that is simple to do, whether on your own or with friends; two symbols indicate where you might need a bit of skill to accomplish it; and three symbols may require a fair bit of practice to get right, or perhaps a few pairs of helping hands to complete.

# CRAFTING

The long evenings of winter can be a drag if you don't
find fun things to occupy yourself with, so here are lots
of suggestions for ways to keep yourself entertained.
There are things to make such as snowflake paper
chains, a papier mâché snowman, a wind chime,
or funny photo albums. Or, why not try some
of the activities specially designed to help you
cope with the wintry weather, such as making
snow shoes or a homemade hand warmer.

# THE ICE HAND

Sometimes you just need a spare hand. Amuse (and frighten) your family and friends with this trick, in which you can make a detachable frozen hand. You can use it for Halloween, in plays or performances, or for other times you want to make people jump.

| | |
|---|---|
| **SKILL LEVEL** | ❄ ❄ |
| **TIME NEEDED** | 1 day |

**1** Using scissors, cut off 3 inches (7.5 cm) from the bottom of the rubber glove so that only the hand, fingers, and a little bit of the wrist section remain.

**2** Using a knife, cut off the top of the soda bottle so that the glove can hang down inside it without touching the bottom.

**3** Push the two wooden skewers into the wrist of the glove to make an "X," and place the glove inside the soda bottle using the skewers for support.

**4** Mix water and food coloring inside a measuring cup. Then fill the rubber glove with the mixture.

**5** Place the glove and its soda-bottle base in the freezer and wait until it freezes—about 5–8 hours.

**6** Remove the frozen hand from the freezer and cut off the rubber glove with your scissors.

## YOU WILL NEED

A pair of scissors

An old rubber glove

A knife

A large empty soda bottle

2 wooden skewers

Water

Food coloring

A measuring cup

A freezer

### DID YOU KNOW?

Although a fairly small part of the body, your hand contains 29 bones, 29 joints, 123 ligaments, 34 muscles, and 48 nerves.

### WARNING

Food coloring will stain carpets, clothes, furniture, and anything else it comes in contact with, so be careful with the frozen hand when it starts to melt.

# SOCK ANIMALS

Hundreds of years ago, puppets and their handlers—known as puppeteers—would travel the countryside putting on puppet shows for a few coins. Kids loved it, but most people considered puppet shows to be a crude and unskilled form of entertainment. The fact is, puppeteers have a very difficult job. They have to act with their hands, and they have to know how to operate lots of different kinds of puppets. Making some of the more complicated puppets is a job better left to professional puppeteers, but you can make a simple sock animal puppet yourself.

| SKILL LEVEL | ❄ |
|---|---|
| TIME NEEDED | ½–1 hour |

## YOU WILL NEED

An old sock

Some colorful felt or cardboard

A pair of scissors

Glue or needle and thread

**1** Place a sock over your hand and tuck part of the toe end in between your thumb and outstretched fingers. This creates a mouth.

**2** Cut out a red or pink triangular piece of cloth for a nose, and two round black bits of cloth for eyes.

**3** Using the mouth as a reference, glue or sew the pieces of cloth onto your sock puppet in the right places to make a face.

**4** To make a snake, cut out a long red tongue and glue or sew it in place inside the mouth. For a dog, bear, or other animal, use a round pink piece as a tongue.

**5** Make triangular ears and attach them to the top.

**6** For a more permanent sock puppet, cut out two pieces of cardboard for the top and bottom parts of the mouth, and then glue them in place.

**7** To make the puppet "talk," simply move your fingers and thumb up and down as if the puppet's mouth were moving.

**8** Make up funny phrases and a silly voice for your puppet, and try cracking some jokes. You can also give yourself a performance space to put on a show by tacking a sheet across a doorway so that you can stand or kneel behind it without your audience being able to see you, and the puppets can perform over the top.

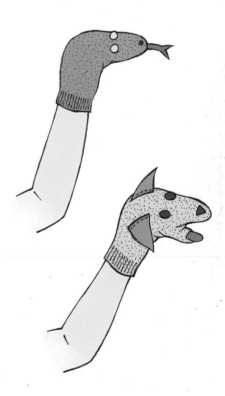

# SHADOW PLAY

Shadow play, or shadow puppets, was invented in the Far East hundreds of years ago and is still very popular in countries like India and Indonesia. It consists of wood, leather, or cardboard cutouts that make shadows on a wall or a white screen.

| | |
|---|---|
| **SKILL LEVEL** | ❄ |
| **TIME NEEDED** | ½ hour |

**1** Draw the outline of your favorite animal on a piece of cardboard. If you aren't a good artist, find a picture on the Internet, print it out, then glue it to the cardboard. Make the puppet at least as large as your open hand, if not larger.

**2** Cut out the puppet following the outline of the animal figure.

**3** Glue a popsicle stick onto the middle of one side of the puppet. This will be your handle.

**4** For a more complicated puppet, make the arms separately and fix them to the puppet's shoulders with paper fasteners. Attach popsicle sticks to the hands so you can move the arms independent of the body.

**5** There are two ways to put on a display with your shadow puppets. One is to shine a lamp onto a white wall and use your puppets to make shadows on it.

**6** The other is to fix up a sheet across a doorway and sit behind it with your puppets and the lamp. Make sure your audience is on the other side. Shine the lamp on the sheet, and use the popsicle sticks to hold the puppets against the lit area—they'll make a silhouette on the other side for your audience to see.

**7** Make multiple characters and get a few friends together to operate them and provide voices. Then you can stage a full play.

## YOU WILL NEED

Cardboard

A pencil

A pair of scissors

Glue

Popsicle sticks

A sheet or white wall

A lamp

# DESIGNING A BOARD GAME

On rainy days indoors, we all love to play board games. Instead of always playing the same old games, why not invent your own? They're great fun to make and, when it's finished, you can play the game with your friends. Board games have been played in most cultures and societies throughout history; some even predate literacy skill development in the earliest civilizations. One of the oldest known board games is called the Senet and was found under Egyptian burials from 3500 B.C.!

| SKILL LEVEL | ✹ ✹ |
| --- | --- |
| TIME NEEDED | 1 hour |

**1** Give some thought to the theme of your game. Is it a path game that's based on luck, such as Snakes and Ladders, or is it a game based on skill, such as Trivial Pursuit? Use your imagination and be as creative as you like.

**2** Roughly outline the rules of the game: How many players? Do you need pieces? How do you win?

**3** Sketch a rough draft of your board design on paper. When you're happy with it, you can draw your final design on the base board.

**4** Now decorate it, making it as bright and colorful as you like.

**5** On thin card such as from cereal boxes, draw out your playing pieces, incorporating an extra ½ inch (1.25 cm) rectangle at the bottom, which you can bend over so that it stands up.

**6** If your game needs cards, such as the Chance cards in Monopoly, you can write the instructions (for example, "Go back 3 spaces") on index cards that have been cut in half. Stack them on the board and trace a line around them. That's where they sit.

**7** Alternatively, write the instructions directly on the board and if you land on that square, you must follow the direction, e.g., "Skip a turn."

**8** If required, use dice or a spinner from another game. Test your design before trying it out on your friends, and then, when you're happy, let the fun begin.

## YOU WILL NEED

Stiff cardboard for the game board

Draft paper

Paints, colored pens and paper, stickers (to decorate)

Thin card (for players)

Dice or spinner

## TOP TIP

Game pieces can be absolutely anything. If you don't want to make customized pieces, you can use coins, small toys, or even the playing pieces from other games.

# SNOWFLAKE PAPER CHAINS

Before we had flashing lights and fancy glass baubles, people decorated their homes with festive, homemade paper chains for the holidays. They're easy to make and, if you want to decorate your own room, they look fun and retro.

| | |
|---|---|
| **SKILL LEVEL** | ❄ |
| **TIME NEEDED** | ½–1 hour |

**1** Fold your sheet of paper in half lengthways and cut it down the middle to make two strips. Attach the strips with tape to make an even longer strip.

**2** Starting at one end, fold the strip like a concertina, back and forth, with the width of the folds about 1–1½ inches (2.5–4 cm).

**3** Place the stack with the folded edge of the top layer on the left. Now use a pencil to trace half a snowflake along the opposite side, making sure the pattern reaches the folded side and that enough of the edges remain intact, about ¼ inch (0.5 cm), so that the chain doesn't fall apart.

**4** Using sharp scissors, carefully cut around the pattern.

**5** Unfold the chain carefully, making sure not to tear any of the parts that join your snowflakes together.

**6** Decorate the snowflakes by tracing thin lines of glue along the branches and sprinkling on silver glitter, or whatever other embellishments you like.

## YOU WILL NEED

**Plain or colored paper or cardboard**

**Adhesive tape**

**A pencil**

**A pair of scissors**

**Glue and glitter (to decorate)**

### TOP TIPS

If you crease the edges of the folds of your concertina, it is easier to cut when the time comes.

You can make the chain as long as you want by joining more strips of paper at the start, but don't make it too long or your concertina will be too thick to cut easily.

# KNITTING A SCARF

You don't even need to know how to knit to make a beautiful scarf. Armed only with some yarn and your hands—and a little patience—you can make cozy scarves for you and your friends.

| SKILL LEVEL | ❄ ❄ |
|---|---|
| TIME NEEDED | 3 hours |

**1** Take your ball of yarn and make a slipknot at the end, and then slip the loop over your thumb. With fingers spread and palm facing you, start by loosely weaving the yarn behind the index finger, over the middle finger, then behind the ring finger and over and back around the pinkie, and then back over the ring

finger, behind the middle finger, over the pointer, and behind and around the thumb, ready for the next row.

**2** Repeat the process until you have two loops around each finger, and the yarn is dangling between the thumb and pointer finger.

**3** Starting with the thumb, pull the bottom loop up over the top loop and continue over the top of your fingertip. Repeat for each of your fingers, moving toward the pinkie.

**4** Then, when you only have one loop on each finger, drape the yarn over the thumb and repeat step one to make another row of loops. Again, pull the bottom loops over your fingertips.

## YOU WILL NEED

**Thick, fluffy yarn**

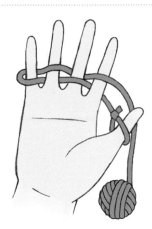

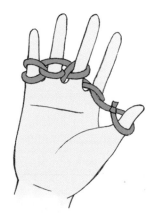

**TOP TIP**

If you want to take a break from "knitting," you can store your work on a stitch holder, a large safety pin, or even a pencil. Then when you are ready to start "knitting" again, you simply put the loops back on your fingers and you're ready to go.

**5** After several rounds, a chain the width of your hand will start to form. When the chain reaches the desired length of your scarf, cut the yarn, leaving a 6–8 inch- (15–20 cm-) long tail.

**6** Weave this tail in and out of each loop before removing the chain from your fingers, being careful not to pull the end too tight or you will squeeze the end of your scarf into a point.

**7** Once the scarf end is the desired shape and tension, then you can tie off with a final knot. The yarn tails at both ends of the scarf can be worked back up through the knitting to neaten it up.

**8** When you have two chains the same length, lay them side by side and weave the edges together by threading yarn back and forth down the middle. Now you have the perfect winter scarf!

# NAPKIN ORIGAMI

At traditional family dinners to celebrate the holidays and festivities, why not entertain your fellow guests by making this simple origami pyramid with your napkin.

| SKILL LEVEL | ❄ |
| --- | --- |
| TIME NEEDED | 15–30 minutes |

## YOU WILL NEED

Linen table napkin

**1** Place a square napkin face down in front of you on the table. Fold the napkin in half along the diagonal, creating a triangle.

**2** Turn the triangle so the longest side forms the base. Now take each bottom corner to meet the point at the top of the triangle. This gives you a napkin diamond.

**3** Now, placing one hand on top of the napkin to secure it and the other underneath, turn it over (left to right), and fold the napkin in half again by folding the top corner down to the bottom corner.

**4** Now, place the fingers of one hand under the central fold and lift it up so that it stands on its two sides, creating an origami napkin.

# MAKING SNOWSHOES

When you're out walking, it can be exhausting if the snow is deep. To stop you from sinking in your boots, you could make yourself a pair of snowshoes that will help you to cross the deeper patches. Snowshoes work by spreading your body weight over a larger area of snow, thus helping you to move more quickly without sinking with every step. Before people built snowshoes, nature provided examples. Several animals, most notably the snowshoe hare, had evolved over the years with oversized feet, enabling them to move more quickly through deep snow.

| | |
|---|---|
| **SKILL LEVEL** | ❄ ❄ ❄ |
| **TIME NEEDED** | 1½–2 hours |

**1** Cut a length of plywood around 20–22 inches long (50–56 cm), and bend it around your knee to make it pliable.

**2** Bend it into an arch and, carefully using your knife (get an adult to help you), scrape away the bark on the inside of the curve to make it more flexible.

**3** Cut one side of both ends of the branch (diagonally), so that when held together, they rest flush against each other.

**4** Hold these ends together and bind with string to form a hoop.

**5** Find six short sticks and bind them in pairs at their center.

**6** Bind the three pairs of sticks across the hoop to support the foot.

**7** Weave string in and around the frame and the cross-sticks to form the base of the snowshoe.

**8** Tie the finished snowshoe to your walking boots with cord.

**9** Then repeat steps one to eight to make one for the other foot.

## YOU WILL NEED

**A length of soft plywood, ¼ in (0.64 cm) thick**

**A sharp knife**

**String**

**Six sticks**

**Cord or bootlaces**

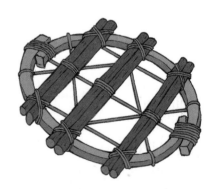

# COZY HAND WARMERS

There's always plenty of fun to be had outside in winter, such as having snowball fights, tobogganing, and making snowmen, but numb, freezing fingers can often bring an end to these games and send us scurrying inside to warm up. Now, with these toastie, homemade hand warmers in your pockets, you'll be able to play in the snow all day long.

| SKILL LEVEL | ❄ ❄ |
|---|---|
| TIME NEEDED | ½ hour |

**1** Cut the wash cloth in half. Keep one half to one side.

**2** Fold the strip in half (right sides facing each other, if applicable), and starting in a corner next to the fold, sew around the pocket, leaving an inch or two on the final side. Turn the bag right side out.

**3** In a bowl, add several drops of your favorite essential oil, or a couple of tablespoons of dried herbs such as lavender or rosemary, to about 1 lb (45 g) rice. Mix well.

**4** Using a small funnel, pour the scented rice into the bag until it's about three-quarters full.

**5** Fold the edges of the filling hole in, and sew them shut.

**6** Make a second bag using the remaining half of the wash cloth, following steps one to five again.

**7** Microwave each bag on medium-high heat for about two minutes.

**8** Your lovely hand warmers should stay hot in your pocket for about a half hour. Once it has lost its warmth, you can go back inside and reheat them.

## YOU WILL NEED

A wash cloth

A pair of scissors

A needle and colored thread (to match wash cloth)

A mixing bowl

Essential oil or dried herbs and spices

Rice

A small funnel

A microwave

## TOP TIP

You can use any type of rice for these warmers—whatever is in the cupboard will do.

# FUNNY PHOTO ALBUMS

After spending a few hours taking photos on a beautiful, clear winter's day (see page 38), it is a shame to just leave them sitting on your computer or phone. Why not continue being creative and make a funny album specifically to store your photos for yourself, or as a gift for a family member or special friend. You can group the photographs in your album by theme, style, and/or chronology.

| | |
|---|---|
| SKILL LEVEL | ❄ |
| TIME NEEDED | 1 hour |

**1** If using digital photographs stored on your computer, print out a selection, or select from any that you may have already printed.

**2** Some photos you may wish to use whole; others you can cut out just the sections that are most fun. Crop them into interesting shapes. Remember to only cut your own photos. If the photo(s) you want to crop belong to other family members, get their permission first.

**3** Punch holes in your colored card to make the desired number of pages for your album.

**4** Using glue, stick as many photos and parts of photos, at crazy angles, onto each sheet.

**5** If you like, you can also write funny captions on the card to accompany some or all of the photos.

**6** Finally, why not personalize the cover of the album too? Glue on fabric, wallpaper, feather, beads, or a photograph—anything that makes the book immediately recognizable, attractive, and significant to whoever you are making it for.

## YOU WILL NEED

Some photographs

A three-ring binder

Colored cardboard (stock paper)

A hole punch

Glue

Colored gel pen

Fabric, wallpaper, beads (to decorate)

# PERSONALIZED GREETINGS CARDS

You can buy some really cute cards for just about every occasion these days, but if you really want to tailor a greeting card for a special event (or a special person), then the best way is to make your own card and put a personal message inside. The festive holiday season is the perfect time to make your own greetings cards.

| | |
|---|---|
| **SKILL LEVEL** | ❄ |
| **TIME NEEDED** | ½–1 hour |

**1** Take a sheet of colored card and fold it in half to make a basic greeting card. Make sure the corners line up before you fold, so that your card doesn't look lopsided.

**2** Find a simple shape that you like and that will appeal to the person who'll be getting the card. Perhaps use the outline of a cat, or a star. You can find images on the Internet or around the house—you can even take them from different-shaped pastry cutters.

**3** Trace the shape and transfer it onto some colored card or stiff paper. Make three copies. Cut them out, decorate them with felt pen or glitter, and then put to one side.

**4** Use felt pens or wiggly strips of colored paper to make a background for your card.

**5** Next, attach the three cutout shapes to the card using glue or double-sided sticky tape. If you can't find a shape you like, try using pressed flowers.

**6** Using a small stamp and ink in different colors, scatter stamped shapes in the spaces between the design. These can be smaller versions of your cutout shapes, or something completely different.

**7** Choose a font you like in a word processing program on your computer. Type and print out a personal message to your friend, then trace it onto your card very lightly. Now draw the final lettering with a colorful, bold felt pen. Now you have a personalized card for any occasion, bound to cheer up whoever is lucky enough to receive it!

## YOU WILL NEED

Thick, good-quality colored paper or greeting card paper (available at craft stores)

Tracing paper

A pair of scissors

Felt pens, glitter, pressed flowers, or other colorful decorations

Thinner colored paper

Glue or double-sided sticky tape

Rubber stamps and ink pads

# BUILDING A LEAF PRESS

Everything in nature happens for a reason and the colors of fall leaves are no different. If you want to preserve some colorful leaves so they don't go brown, you can build a press. Leaves are green because they contain a substance called chlorophyll, which they use to capture sunlight. A tree spends a lot of energy making more chlorophyll for its leaves so it can continue to grow. During winter, trees will stop making chlorophyll and hibernate to conserve their energy for the spring. When the tree stops replenishing chlorophyll, the green color goes out of the leaves and other colors start to show through. The yellow-brown, red, and purple colors come from chemicals already in the leaf. They are always there—we just can't see it the rest of the time because the green chlorophyll usually covers it up.

| SKILL LEVEL | ❄ ❄ |
| --- | --- |
| TIME NEEDED | 1–2 hours |

**YOU WILL NEED**

Two pieces of plywood at least 6 in (15 cm) wide on each side

Tissue paper

Colorful leaves

Two clamps (or a large pile of heavy books)

**1** Lay one of the boards flat on a table and cover it with three or four layers of tissue paper. Make sure there are no wrinkles or creases in the paper, and it's as smooth as possible.

**2** Choose your favorite leaves and lay them on the tissue paper. Leave at least a ½-in (1-cm) gap between neighboring leaves.

**3** Cover the leaves with another three or four layers of tissue paper. Make sure it stays smooth. Put the other board on top.

**4** Finally, either screw clamps tightly at each end of the boards, or pile plenty of heavy books or even bricks on top.

**5** Leave the whole setup in a cool, dry place and the moisture will be squeezed out of the leaves and drawn into the tissue paper. After a few weeks, you will be left with dried-out, flattened leaves, with the fall colors preserved.

**DID YOU KNOW?**

The world's largest leaves come from the Raffia palm. They can grow up to 80 feet (25 m) long!

# MAKING A BIRD FEEDER

Birdwatching is a lot of fun, and since it can be difficult for birds to find food at all times in the colder months, making a bird feeder can double as an attraction for lots of hungry birds, and as a device for you to spot some species that only come out in the winter. And, this pretty bird feeder is not only completely eco-friendly, but biodegradable too!

**SKILL LEVEL** ❄ ❄

**TIME NEEDED** 1 hour

**1** Once you have decided where in the yard is safe to hang your bird feeder, you can then cut the string to the right length.

**2** Tie the string securely around the top of your pinecone.

**3** In a mixing bowl, combine about two cups of seeds and oats.

**4** Using the popsicle stick, spread peanut butter thickly over the pinecone, making sure all the surfaces are well covered and all gaps are filled.

**5** Now roll the buttered pinecone in the seed and oat mixture, pressing down firmly to ensure the mixture sticks to the entire surface.

**6** Using the attached string, hang the pinecone securely from a tree, and enjoy watching the birds as they eat!

## YOU WILL NEED

String

A small mixing bowl

Bird seed, shelled sunflower seeds, or rolled oats

A popsicle stick

Peanut butter

A large pinecone

### WARNING

Birds have lots of predators, including cats, so hang the bird feeder where they can feed without fear of being caught.

### TOP TIP

Make sure the string is securely tied to the cone and to the tree, and that it can hold the weight of the birds as they feed.

# SNAKE DRAFT STOPPER

Snowy weather may make for pretty pictures, but it's not much fun if your bedroom is drafty. Here's how to make a simple but attractive snake draft stopper to keep the cold weather at bay.

| | |
|---|---|
| **SKILL LEVEL** | ❄ ❄ |
| **TIME NEEDED** | 1 hour |

**1** Fold the rectangle of material in half lengthways, so that the pattern is on the inside. Pin along the long side.

**2** Stitch up the long side of the rectangle, as close to the edges as possible.

**3** Turn the material inside out so you have a long tube that is open at both ends, with the pretty side of your fabric on the outside. At one end, fold the two ends in, and sew to make a neat finish.

**4** Cut a leg off your pantyhose and fill it with stuffing. Once it is full and just a bit smaller than your draft stopper, tie a knot in the end.

**5** Insert the stuffed tight leg into the material cover, and stitch the open end together neatly.

**6** To make the snake's head, sew on two buttons on the top for eyes.

**7** Cut a short length of red ribbon and cut a V-shape out of one end to make a forked tongue. Sew onto snake.

## YOU WILL NEED

A rectangular piece of material, at least 16 in (40 cm) wide and 1½ in (4 cm) longer than the width of your door

Pins, a needle, and some thread

A pair of scissors

An old pair of pantyhose

Filling (beanbag balls, lentils, rice)

Two buttons

A red ribbon

### TOP TIP

You can cut off the leg of an old pair of pants and start at step four if you like.

# PAPIER MÂCHÉ SNOWMAN

Just because you're stuck inside or there's no snow outside doesn't mean you can't have the enjoyment of making a snowman. Making a papier mâché snowman is glorious, messy fun, so roll up your sleeves, put on an apron and get to work! The Chinese were the first to invent paper, so it makes sense that they were the first to invent papier mâché. The modern name comes from French and means "chewed paper." Supposedly, French workers in English paper shops would chew on paper to moisten it so they could make papier mâché constructions. It is a great material for constructing things because it is easy to work with, is lightweight, and can be painted.

| | |
|---|---|
| SKILL LEVEL | ❄ ❄ |
| TIME NEEDED | 2 days |

## YOU WILL NEED

All-purpose flour

Water

A large mixing bowl

Salt

Two balloons

Strips of newspaper

Masking tape

White poster paint

Stickers, paint, markers (to decorate)

Black and colored cardboard or felt for hat and scarf

Sticking tape

**1** First, you need to make your papier mâché mixture. Mix one part flour to about two parts water in a large mixing bowl. You're going for the consistency of gravy—not too thick and not too watery. If it's too thick, the paste is difficult to work with. If it's too watery, it will take your project forever to dry.

**2** Add in a tablespoon of salt for each part flour. This helps prevent mold from growing on your models. Stir the mixture until you get all the lumps out.

**3** Blow up one balloon. Then blow up the second one, but make sure it is slightly smaller.

**4** Brush the papier mâché mixture onto each balloon and add strips of newspaper until each one is completely covered. Leave them to dry overnight.

**5** Using masking tape, attach the smaller papier mâché balloon to the bigger balloon—you will see that your snowman is beginning to take shape.

**6** Cover the entire snowman with a second layer of papier mâché mixture and strips of newspaper. Allow to dry thoroughly and then paint white.

**7** Using stickers, or cutting out pieces of colored paper, add a row of buttons to the front of your snowman's body plus some eyes, a nose, and a mouth to his head.

**8** To make his hat, cut a strip of black card about 2–3 inches (5–7.5 cm) wide and roll into a cylinder. Secure with tape.

**9** Using a piece of black card, trace around the circle of the cylinder and cut out. This is the top of the hat.

**10** Find a bigger circle to draw around, such as a small plate, and attach to the base of the cylinder to make the rim of the hat. Attach to the snowman's head.

**11** Use a strip of colored card or craft felt to make his scarf–the finishing touch!

## PAPER CANOES

A form of papier mâché was used in the nineteenth century to make canoes. That might not sound advisable, but it meant that they were much lighter and could thus be carried from place to place. Because the paper sheets could be printed at any length, it allowed the boat hull to be one continuous piece, without any seams. Not many of these boats have survived today, but one of the best known is the Maria Theresa, which was sailed down the east coast of the United States in the nineteenth century by Nathaniel H. Bishop, who published his travels in a book called *Voyage of the Paper Canoe*.

# CREATING A COMIC STRIP

If you're good at drawing, you can keep yourself and your friends amused by creating a comic strip.

| SKILL LEVEL | ❄ ❄ |
|---|---|
| TIME NEEDED | 1–2 hours |

**YOU WILL NEED**

A pencil, pen, and/or slim black marker

Paper

**1** Experiment with drawing some characters. These can be human, aliens, animals, or objects that come to life–whatever you like. Then think about their characters and possible names.

**2** Think of a short, humorous tale or a joke and mentally break it into sections. Now create a rough image for each section and quickly sketch it, using stick figures, or quick drawings.

**3** Think of a title and captions, if any–a comic strip can be a purely visual joke if you prefer.

**4** Now draw your good copy, with characters drawn in full and all details and color added. Then show the final version to your friends and see if it makes them laugh!

# PLASTER CAST MOLDINGS

It's easy to make plaster of Paris shapes which you can use for jewelry, to decorate your bedroom walls, or as paper weights. And, be as imaginative as you like when it comes to decorating your creations.

SKILL LEVEL ❄ ❄ ❄

TIME NEEDED 1–2 hours

**1** Grease the ice cube tray or mold using a little petroleum jelly on your finger.

**2** Using a measuring cup, measure an ounce of plaster of Paris powder into the disposable bowl. Thoroughly mix with one cup of water, making sure you get rid of any lumps.

**3** Add some colored poster paint to the mixture. Stir slowly until the color is consistent and to your liking.

**4** Put on your gloves and carefully pour the mixture into the ice cube tray or candy mold. Shake the molds to make sure the mixture settles completely and there are no air pockets.

**5** Allow to set. This could take anything from a few minutes to an hour, depending on the size of the objects.

**6** When the plaster is nearly dry, delicately remove the shape from the mold.

**7** Depending on whether you want to string them together with beads to make bracelets or to turn them into paper weights, you can decorate your shapes however you like.

## YOU WILL NEED

Flexible ice cube trays or candy shape molds

Some petroleum jelly

A measuring cup

Powdered plaster of Paris (available from craft shops)

A disposable mixing bowl

1 cup (250 ml) water

Some colored poster paint

A spoon

Rubber gloves

## TOP TIPS

If the mixture starts to dry up while you're still mixing, simply add a drop more water.

Getting your shapes out of the molds is the hardest part of the whole process. Test the shape with your fingertips; when it's only slightly moist, it's ready to remove.

# MAKING A SNOW GLOBE

Have you ever wondered how they get the snow inside a snow globe? In this project, you will discover how to do exactly that so that you can create your own winter landscape.

**SKILL LEVEL**                            ❄ ❄

**TIME NEEDED**              45 minutes–1 hour

**1** Take the poster putty, mold it into a disk, and put it in the bottom of the jar. The tack will represent the ice.

**2** On your paper, draw a skating figure or a snowman, or anything you like that will make a good wintery scene—remember that your picture needs to be small enough to fit in the jar. Put your plastic over the drawing and trace your drawing with the marker.

**3** Paint your figures on the plastic and allow them to dry. Cut out the shapes, leaving a long strip at the top of the figures—this will be used to attach the figures to the top of the jar.

**4** Pour the water into the jar and add about two teaspoons of glycerine and five teaspoons of glitter.

**5** Using tape, stick your cutout figures onto the inside of the jar lid.

**6** Screw the lid back on and secure with a tight rubber band. Shake to watch the snow fall.

## YOU WILL NEED

**Some reusable poster putty**

**A screw-top jar with as wide an opening as possible**

**A sheet of 8½ x 11 in paper**

**A pencil**

**A piece of transparent plastic (the type that food containers are made from), not too thick**

**A black permanent marker pen**

**Acrylic paints**

**A fine paintbrush**

**A pair of scissors**

**Water**

**A teaspoon**

**Glycerine, available from the drugstore**

**Silver or white glitter**

**Clear tape**

**A rubber band**

# MAKING A WIND CHIME

Modern wind chimes have their origins in Indian wind bells. They used to be hung on the corners of pagodas (tiered towers) with the purpose of scaring away birds and evil spirits. Later, these wind bells were introduced to China and were also hung in temples, palaces, and homes. In *feng shui* (the Chinese practice of choosing and arranging work and living spaces to promote balance and comfort), wind chimes are used to attract good luck to the home. You can make this beautiful wind chime more generic, or give it a real wintry feel with items that conjure up feelings of winter.

| SKILL LEVEL | ❄ ❄ |
| TIME NEEDED | 1–2 hours |

## YOU WILL NEED

Small bells

Bright beads of different shapes, sizes, and materials (some of wood, clay, glass)

Pretty pebbles

Small winter-themed ornaments (if using)

A pair of scissors

A string or nylon thread (such as fishing line)

Clear-drying glue

A skewer or a scissor blade

A round lid from a plastic container (such as a margarine tub)

Brightly colored yarn/wool

**1** Select eight or ten items from your collections of beads, bells, and pebbles, and/or winter-themed ornaments that you'd like to hang on your wind chime.

**2** Cut string or nylon thread into lengths about 6 inches (15 cm) each.

**3** Thread the string through the holes in your objects. (If you can't find shells with natural holes in them, you could ask an adult to drill small holes in them using an electric drill.)

**4** For heavier items such as pebbles, wrap the string around the object several times, then rub glue on the string and pebble to hold it in place. Allow to dry.

**5** Using a skewer or scissor blade, carefully poke small holes evenly around the edge of the plastic lid.

**6** Pull the pieces of string through the holes and then tie a knot at each end so it can't slip back through.

**7** Punch two holes in the middle of the plastic lid.

**8** Loop a length of yarn through both holes and tie a knot. This is to hang your wind chime.

**9** Hang your wind chime either inside a window or near a door so it can tinkle and chime as it catches the breeze.

## TOP TIP

If the items on your wind chime are small, you can always hang several on each string.

# NATURE COLLAGE

The next time you go on a walk, why not collect some nature specimens and trinkets that you can then use to make a stunning collage at home. Look out for things that are especially associated with fall and winter including seasonal flowers, berries, twigs, and leaves.

**SKILL LEVEL** ❄

**TIME NEEDED** ½–1 hour

**1** A great way to set off a nature collage is to give it a natural background, instead of just plain paper. First, spread a thin layer of glue all over your construction paper or sheet of card.

**2** Sprinkle with collected local sand or gravel to form a base layer. If you want to give the collage a snow-like look, you can also sprinkle the paper with a layer of icing sugar on top.

**3** Once the glue is dry, it is ready for you to start your collage.

**4** Choose the objects that you want to use. Before gluing anything down, first arrange your collage on the background, to make sure you are happy with the way it looks.

**5** Once you are happy with your arrangement, spread a little glue under each item and replace firmly on the card.

**6** Once the glue has dried completely, attach the cord or string to the back of the collage using strong tape so that it hangs without any danger of falling.

## YOU WILL NEED

Glue

Construction paper or card

Sand or gravel (optional)

Icing sugar (optional)

Collected items (leaves, twigs, dry moss, flowers, seeds, seedpods)

Cord or string, to hang

Strong tape

# OUTDOOR PLAY

When the fall colors start to fade and the dark nights of winter shorten the afternoons, it's tempting to go indoors and hibernate like sleepy bears until the spring flowers start to bloom. What's more, there is something inviting about curling up around a fireplace with a cup of hot chocolate and a good book. But, just because it's cold outside doesn't mean you can't enjoy the outdoors. In fact, the colder weather calls for an array of exciting activites, projects, and sports you just can't do in summer. Pretty soon, you'll be glad it's winter.

# HIKING

Every explorer, from Magellan to Indiana Jones, has had to know how to use a compass and read a map. In dire situations, many have even found their way without any tools, using shadows and the stars to guide them on their adventures. Whether you're setting out to conquer Mount Kilimanjaro or the hill behind your house, knowing how to get there—and get home—is a great skill to have. Once you work out how to use a map and compass, it'll be easy. Getting started, however, is a little complicated. After two or three outings you should have cracked it.

## READING A MAP

The basic tools for finding where you are and where you're going are a map and a compass (see page 36). You can probably already find your way with a road map, but it's a bit harder to use a map with no roads on it. You can pick up a local map from tourist centers or park stations.

**1** First, you'll notice that these kinds of maps have a grid of lines over the top of them as if someone was dividing the map up into squares. The up-and-down lines are north and south. The left-to-right lines are east and west.

**2** On some roadless maps you'll also notice lots of winding, curving lines on the map. These are called contour lines and they tell you how the land drops off (for gorges or river beds) and rises up (for hills and mountains).

**3** All maps have detailed legends or keys that will tell you what all the colors and lines mean. By referring to the key you can tell what kinds of trees, fields, and rocks you can expect to find.

**4** Check the scale on the map when you plan your route—a 1:50,000 map scale means the map area is 50,000 times smaller than the real area, so a distance of 1 inch (2.5 cm) on the map is 50,000 inches (125,000 cm), or about 0.8 miles (1.25 km).

| SKILL LEVEL | ❄ |
|---|---|
| TIME NEEDED | 1 hour |

**YOU WILL NEED**

A map

**WARNING**

Always make sure someone responsible knows where you're going so they can find you in case you get lost.

# HAPPY HIKING

So, now you know which direction you're going in, but do you know how to get to your destination without blisters and still in high spirits? Well, here are a few tips on happy hiking. You need to be prepared for changeable weather conditions, so a backpack with an extra layer and some waterproof clothing is essential. You should also be able to find your way back home, so make sure you familiarize yourself with map reading before you set out on your adventure.

### YOU WILL NEED

Outdoor clothing

Walking shoes or hiking boots

**1** Check the weather beforehand, because it gives you a better idea of what's involved without having to contend unprepared with wind and rain.

**2** It's a good idea at first to go with experienced hikers. If you don't have any hiking friends or family, join an organized group until you've got the hang of things—the local library is a good place to find details. Once you have some group hiking experience under your belt, you can start to go for longer and more challenging hikes.

**3** Always wear comfortable clothes that are designed for the job. And don't worry that you'll look like a dork—there's some really great-looking outdoor gear available now. Take water and high-energy snacks with you. And don't forget the warm clothes.

**4** Don't wear brand-new footwear on a hike or you'll end up with blisters. Wear your shoes around town until they're comfortable, and then start with short, easy hikes to get your muscles used to walking longer distances.

**5** Plan your route together with your hiking group—something that you agree is achievable.

**6** Pack your kit—map, compass, water, energy snacks—and you're ready to go.

# MAKING A COMPASS

Invented in China over 1,000 years ago, compasses use the Earth's magnetic field to tell you which way is north. Movement of lava beneath the Earth's crust creates a very weak magnetic field running between the planet's North and South Poles. A very light magnetic needle, if it's allowed to swing freely, will align itself with this field, because the poles on magnets attract and repel each other. This means the needle will always swing around to point north, no matter how you turn it. Unfortunately, there are times we forget to pack a real compass, but not to worry—you can make one. Fortunately, the Earth's magnetic field is strong enough to attract magnetized sewing needles or paper clips, if they're given freedom to spin by being floated on water. Here's how to set up your own so you can always tell which way is north.

| | |
|---|---|
| SKILL LEVEL | ❄ ❄ |
| TIME NEEDED | 15 minutes |

**1** Run the magnet slowly over the needle about ten times, making sure you do so in the same direction each time. This will make the needle magnetic enough to act as a compass.

**2** If you don't have a magnet, you can still magnetize your needle or paper clip using static electricity. You can use material from a nylon raincoat or fleece jacket to build up the charge. Simply stroke the needle in the same direction with the material you have on hand. You need to do this at least fifty times.

**3** Fill a plastic container with water, and then gently place a leaf or large blade of grass on the water's surface, so it floats on top in the center of the container.

**4** Then carefully place the magnetized needle on top of the floating leaf or blade of grass, so that it floats freely on the surface of the water.

**5** Watch as the needle will then turn to point itself toward the North Pole.

## YOU WILL NEED

A magnet

A plastic container to hold water

Water

A leaf or large blade of grass

A small piece of metal, like a needle, paper clip, or small nail

### WARNING

This method won't work if you use a bowl made from metal to hold the water. The magnetized needle will be attracted to the metal bowl insead of swinging freely to point north.

**6** Try to test your homemade compass in a place that's sheltered from the wind. Earth's magnetic poles might be strong enough to attract a magnetized needle, but that doesn't say much. A breeze, even a gentle one, can easily push your leaf off course.

**7** Of course, this will only show you a line between north and south. You need some other clues to work out which is which. The sun is one clue: in the northern hemisphere, the sun will always be in the southern half of the sky, on the eastern side in the morning and the western side in the evening. In the southern hemisphere, the sun will always be on the northern side of the sky.

## DID YOU KNOW?

You've heard of north, south, east, and west, but did you know old-time sailors divided the compass into thirty-two points? There are seven points between north and east: northeast is halfway between the two; north-northeast is halfway between north and northeast; north-by-east is halfway between north-northeast; and so on. A diagram showing all thirty-two points is called a "compass rose." Modern compasses are divided into 360 degrees, for even more accurate measurements.

# COLLECTING WATER

A long day of hiking will surely make you thirsty, so you will need to find a water source. But, if you can't find one, you can always collect water for yourself during a storm or rain shower.

| | |
|---|---|
| **SKILL LEVEL** | ❄ |
| **TIME NEEDED** | 30 minutes |

## YOU WILL NEED

**Plastic sheeting**

**2 long straight sticks**

**2 shorter sticks**

**String**

**A heavy stone**

**1** Lay your plastic sheeting on the ground and mark out the points where the corners lie.

**2** Push two long sticks into the ground at the back corners and two shorter sticks at the front corners. Drape the sheeting over the sticks so it sits off the ground and forms a slope.

**3** Poke a small hole in the middle of the sheeting at the lower end. Tie a piece of string to this hole and tuck the other end under a heavy stone on the ground. This pulls the middle of the front of the sheet down to make a sort of spout, down which the collected rainwater will run. Put a container under this spout and as soon as it rains, you'll have cold, running water.

# WINTER PHOTOGRAPHY

Winter can be a great time to try your hand at photography. The crisp light of a sunny December morning makes colors sing, while seasonal wonders like icicles and snowfall seem as pristine as freshly laid paint. Days like these are the perfect time to dig out your camera and start snapping. Years ago, photography was a very skilled hobby, but modern technology means it is now much easier to get good results. Even a basic digital camera can be used to take impressive pictures that you can share with your friends in print or on a computer. Get in the habit of taking a camera with you on walks and trips outside and soon enough you'll spot something striking or beautiful that deserves to have its picture taken. When you do, all you'll need to do is take your camera from your pocket and capture the moment.

| SKILL LEVEL | ❄ ❄ |
| --- | --- |
| TIME NEEDED | 1 hour |

**YOU WILL NEED**

A camera

A computer (optional)

**1** On a day when the light is strong and clear, go outside with your camera. Look for a special feature that catches the eye. It could be a fir tree with a blanket of snow on its branches, or icicles hanging from a ledge.

**2** Looking through the viewfinder of the camera, or the digital viewing screen its rear, carefully frame the feature you are interested in. Get as close to the subject as you can while still keeping all of the features you want inside the shot.

**3** If possible, it's better to have the sun shining from behind you when you take the picture. That way, the object you want to photograph will be well lit and your camera will not be "dazzled" by light shining directly at it from in front.

**4** If you are taking a picture of a landscape, make sure the horizon is straight rather than tilted in the viewfinder. Some experts think that positioning the viewfinder so that land fills two thirds of the frame and sky fills the last third (or vice versa) makes for a good picture—try both ways and see if you agree.

**5** After you have taken your pictures, it's time to view them. If you have a digital camera, you can look at the images right away on a home computer, provided you have the correct connecting cable. Ask an adult to help if you're not sure. If you also have a printer on hand, you can buy special photographic paper that will allow you to make high-quality prints of your pictures at home.

**6** Alternatively, you can take your camera to a professional photography store with printing facilities. Ask the staff to help you choose what kind of prints to have made. This will cost money, so get permission from an adult first.

## THE GOLDEN RATIO

The Golden Ratio is a guideline that can be used for the composition of photographs, to draw the human eye into the composition, based on the ratio of placement of the different elements in the picture. It is a constant, often expressed as 1.618 (although this is what is known as an irrational number—the digits after the decimal point go on forever).

In 1509, an Italian mathematician Luca Pacioli, published a book called *De Divina Proportione*. The book covered how proportions were used not only in math but also in art and architecture. Following the publication, many Renaissance painters and architects used the Golden Ratio in their works, including Leonardo da Vinci, believing it to be aesthetically pleasing.

Imagine you have a straight line divided into two parts, one longer length (*a*) and one shorter length (*b*). The Golden Ratio is when the ratio of *b* to *a* is the same as the ratio of *a* to the whole line. So if *a* is about 1.618 times greater than *b*, you've divided it in the Golden Ratio.

### DID YOU KNOW?

That the first photographs were taken more than 170 years ago? French scientist Louis Daguerre took the first picture of a person in 1839, with a very basic film camera that took several minutes to capture an image after the button was pressed—so the person in the picture had to stay very still.

# BUILDING A SNOW FORTRESS

Every good polar explorer needs a fortress to protect them from wild creatures and icy winds. And, if you can make a snowman, you can build a snow fortress, because both activities involve the same basic techniques. A fortress makes an ideal outpost from which to hurl snow at opponents during snowball fights, you can use it as a base camp for an outdoor expedition (see page 44), or whatever else captures your imagination. It helps to have a few people to help out, as this activity takes a little time.

| | |
|---|---|
| SKILL LEVEL | ❄ ❄ |
| TIME NEEDED | 2 hours |

**1** Start making a large ball of snow by first making a small one with your hands and rolling it over and over through fresh snow. Pat it down with your hands to firm up the shape, and continue adding bulk until the ball stands waist high.

**2** After you have made at least three giant snow balls (depending on how big you want your fort), pack them together side by side to make a wall. Repeat the process until you have made the four walls of your fortress, filling in any gaps with loose snow as you go. Remember to leave a gap in one of the walls so you can get in and out.

**3** Make a few smaller balls of snow to add on top of the walls to build it up to the desired height. Use a pump-action sprayer filled with water to turn surfaces to ice and bind blocks together.

**4** If you wish, you can make your fort into a larger structure by adding linking passages and battlements. Add a flagpole so you can fly the emblem of your expedition above the fort (even if it is only an old dishcloth!).

## YOU WILL NEED

Lots of fresh snow

A few helpers

A pump-action sprayer

Water

### DID YOU KNOW?

The Snow Castle of Kemi, in Finland, is the largest snow structure in the world. Rebuilt from scratch every year, it measures between 139,931 and 215,278 square feet (13,000 and 20,000 square meters), and you can even stay there overnight in a special ice hotel!

# BUILDING A CAMPFIRE

If you're enjoying the great outdoors, you may need to build a fire to keep warm. Building a fire takes real skill and care. Where you locate the fire is as important as how you build it. Fires should be in areas that are relatively out of the wind and well away from low-hanging limbs and dry grasses.

| | |
|---|---|
| **SKILL LEVEL** | ✳ ✳ |
| **TIME NEEDED** | ½ hour |

**1** Clear a circle about 6 feet (2 m) in diameter of any undergrowth, and scrape it down until you reach bare soil. Then dig a shallow fire pit at the center of the circle and surround it with rocks. This makes sure you only burn what you mean to—the basic rule of fire safety.

**2** Put your bundle of tinder at the center of your fire pit. Use pencil-sized pieces of kindling to make a small teepee over the tinder bed.

**3** Build the teepee out using gradually larger and larger pieces of wood. Don't use pieces of wood that are fatter than your wrist, or you'll risk the teepee collapsing. Finish off with four larger logs in a square.

**4** Once the teepee is finished, light the tinder at its center.

## YOU WILL NEED

Some rocks

A cricket-ball-sized bundle of tinder, like dried grass, wood shavings, or even bits of fur

Pencil-sized twigs and sticks

Medium-sized sticks/pieces of wood

Four large logs

Matches

**WARNING**

Always make sure there is an adult present to supervise any activity involving building or lighting a fire.

# LIGHTING A FIRE WITHOUT MATCHES

Modern matches were invented in England in 1827 by a man named John Walker. Before that, anyone who wanted to start a fire had to do it without matches, either by striking sparks from flint or rubbing two sticks together. The Native Americans devised a technique called "the bow and drill" in which they used a bow, similar to the bows they used with arrows only much smaller, and a long piece of wood to "drill" into another piece of wood called the hearth. The friction between the drill and hearth creates enough heat to ignite fur, dried grass and leaves, and other tinder. It's not easy, but it will work as long as you're willing to find the right materials and put some energy into the drilling. This technique works best when the drill, and the hearth are dry, and made of the same type of wood.

| SKILL LEVEL | ❋ ❋ ❋ |
| --- | --- |
| TIME NEEDED | 1 hour |

## YOU WILL NEED

A teepee of tinder and kindling

A knife

A straight stick of hardwood for the drill

A flat piece of dry hardwood for the hearth

A hand-sized piece of hardwood to use as the socket (this is what you'll hold to press down on the drill when you're turning it)

A cord, shoelace, or any other length of tough string

A 1-ft-(30-cm-) long stick of flexible wood for the bow

A strong piece of bark

Tinder

**1** Before starting, make sure you're positioned close to your teepee of tinder and kindling. Once you get an ember, you'll need to transfer it quickly to the fire.

**2** Start making your bow and drill by whittling one end of the drill into a point. Round off the other end.

**3** Cut a small hole halfway along the hearth about 1 inch (2.5 cm) from an edge. The hole should be big enough to allow the rounded end of the drill to fit inside it.

**4** Next, cut a triangular notch in the hearth from the hole to the

nearest edge. This will serve as a channel for ashes and embers to spill out onto your tinder.

**5** You're going to use the socket to press down firmly on the drill. To stop it from slipping, cut a small hole in the socket so that the rounded end of the drill will fit there snugly.

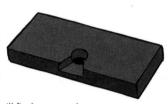

**6** Tie the cord or shoelace to the bow. It's helpful to find a bow stick that's already bent, but a freshly cut stick should bend as you tie on the cord.

**7** Place the hearth on the ground so that the notched side is in contact with a small but strong piece of bark (this is where you will collect the embers).

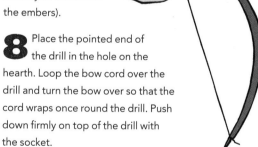

**8** Place the pointed end of the drill in the hole on the hearth. Loop the bow cord over the drill and turn the bow over so that the cord wraps once round the drill. Push down firmly on top of the drill with the socket.

**9** Make sawing motions with the bow to work the drill back and forth in a not-too-fast, not-too-slow, steady rhythm. Make sure the drill stays in contact with the hearth. This gets tiring, so you may want a parent or a friend to take a turn.

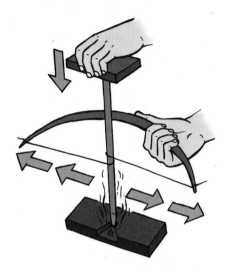

**10** Eventually the friction will cause smoke to form, and dark brown smoking powder should start rolling down the notch and onto the bark. When smoke appears, increase speed and pressure on the drill.

**11** Once the notch is filled with smoking powder and the powder is smoking on its own, gently move the hearth away from the bark and smoking powder. Place the smoking powder onto a small but tight ball of tinder, and blow on it until it turns into a glowing red ember. The tinder should also begin to catch fire.

**12** Quickly take the smoldering ball of tinder to the teepee of tinder and kindling, and place it gently on the tinder platform. Blow on it more if need be until the kindling catches.

**WARNING**

Always make sure there is an adult present to supervise any activity involving building or lighting a fire.

# OUTDOOR EXPEDITIONS

Some of the most dramatic and daring tales of real-life adventure belong to the polar explorers. You can follow in their footsteps by mounting your own outdoor expedition. Explorers of a century ago braved ice and hunger to find the North Pole. But a trek across the countryside to "discover" a goal such as a monument or lake is much more fun—and hopefully will still present a few challenges that will test your mettle as an explorer. Below are some explorer skills you can try along the way.

| SKILL LEVEL | ❄ ❄ |
| --- | --- |
| TIME NEEDED | 2 hours |

## MAKE A DEBRIS SHELTER

The elements themselves were the biggest danger faced by explorers. In addition to weatherproof clothing, they needed shelters to protect them from the wind, snow, and cold temperatures. Here's a makeshift debris shelter you can make using natural materials, no matter what the weather is.

**1** First, find a large rock or tree stump and a sturdy branch to act as your ridge pole, which should be a few feet taller than you. This will form the backbone of the shelter.

**2** Brace your ridge pole firmly against the rock or tree stump. Find other sturdy sticks and branches, and tie them together to form two side sticks. The tied ends of the sticks will be used to hold your ridge pole in place, and the other ends will extend down to the ground. You will now have a tripod-like structure. It should be big enough to hold two explorers.

**3** Line the ridge pole with more sticks. After this, gather as much debris as you can find and thatch your whole shelter with it. Use whatever the surrounding area offers: leaves, pine needles, dried ferns, grass, mud, etc.

**4** Real explorers kept a record of the things they saw so people could learn from their discoveries. While you are on your expedition, make notes about the weather conditions, the animals, and any difficulties you encountered along the way.

### YOU WILL NEED

A large rock or tree stump

A sturdy branch for your ridge pole

Various sizes of branches and sticks

Debris

A notebook and pen

### DID YOU KNOW?

The first explorer to reach the North Pole was American Navy engineer Robert Edwin Peary in 1909—although he lost eight toes to frostbite during the attempt and was later dogged by claims that he didn't fully complete the journey to the Pole itself. Some believe a fellow American explorer, Dr. Frederick Cook, reached the North Pole a year before Peary—and the controversy still lingers today.

# SPOTTING WILDLIFE

At first glance the winter landscape can seem bleak and lifeless. But watch carefully and you'll find many animals going about their business in the snow. All you need to know is where to look. Some animals, like bears, hibernate all the way through winter. Others, like squirrels, venture out at regular intervals to look for something to eat. They bury stores of acorns and nuts earlier in the year that they can depend on during winter when food is scarce. Some bird species migrate south to warmer countries, where conditions are less harsh. Many birds remain at home in winter, though, and the absence of leaves in the trees makes them easier to spot when perched than in summer.

| | |
|---|---|
| **SKILL LEVEL** | ❄ |
| **TIME NEEDED** | 1 hour |

1 Identify a place to look for wildlife. Nature reserves are best, but plenty of animals can be seen even in your own backyard.

2 Find a quiet, comfortable place to watch from—like a window overlooking a garden, or a sheltered spot outdoors near a natural feature that attracts wildlife, such as a lake or woods.

3 Sit still and watch carefully. If you have binoculars, use them to scan the bare branches of trees—you'll often find birds hopping around. Look carefully near thickets too, as shy animals like foxes often forage beside these sheltered areas.

4 Record what you see on a notepad. If you don't recognize some of the wildlife you encounter, describe its features and behavior instead: How big is it? What is its shape and color? Does it hop, fly, or crawl? Is it fast or slow moving? These details will help you identify it in a book later.

5 Before you leave, note down the location, time, and weather conditions of your visit. That way, if you return to the same spot throughout the year, you can build up a detailed record of how the passing seasons influence wildlife.

## YOU WILL NEED

- A pair of binoculars (optional, but helpful)
- A notepad and pen

# MAKING A SNOWMAN

There's nothing more exciting than the first snowfall of the winter: the soft white carpet that's replaced the green of your backyard, the gentle fall of nature's pure white flakes, and of course, the chance to build a snowman that will be the envy of your neighborhood. Just like sandcastles, there's a right and a wrong way to build a snowman. The first thing you need for the perfect snowman is the right kind of snow—not too fluffy, not too icy—but that all depends on what Mother Nature has in store, so you'll just have to make the best of what you have.

| SKILL LEVEL | ❄ ❄ |
|---|---|
| TIME | ½ hour |

**1** Choose your building site—preferably somewhere clearly visible and surrounded by plenty of snow so that you have all the materials you need.

**2** Make a reasonably sized snowball, then roll it along the ground to pick up more snow to add to its size. Keep going until you have a ball that is 1–3 feet (0.3–0.9 meters) in diameter. This will be your snowman's lower body.

**3** Repeat for the upper body and the head, although both of these should be smaller than the first ball. Then, attach these to the top of the largest snowball so you have a large (lower body), medium (upper body), and small (head) ball. Make sure these are attached properly as there's nothing as sad as a decapitated snowman.

**4** Make the nose with a carrot, eyes with pebbles or pieces of coal, and a mouth with smaller pebbles. A hat and a scarf are obligatory clothing. Then stand back and enjoy the acclaim from your family and friends.

## YOU WILL NEED

Plenty of snow

A carrot

Pebbles

Pieces of coal

Assortment of old winter clothing (scarf, hat, gloves)

# ICE FISHING

When a deep freeze sets in for weeks, a thick layer of ice forms over lakes. But beneath the ice, fishes still swim in the depths—meaning that, with care, it may be possible to go ice fishing. Before you begin, you must be absolutely sure the ice is thick enough to walk on safely. Venturing onto ice that is not thick enough is extremely dangerous and should never be attempted—if you are not sure, it is far better to stay off the ice altogether. Always go with an adult, and let others know where you are going and when you plan to return. Check the safety tips on the opposite page for ways to spot whether the ice is safe to walk on. If conditions are right, you can set off for a day's fishing. You'll need a special shortened ice fishing rod and some lures and a hand augur (drill) to make a hole in the ice through which to fish.

| SKILL LEVEL | ❄ ❄ ❄ |
| --- | --- |
| TIME NEEDED | 3 hours |

## YOU WILL NEED

Warm, waterproof clothes and shoes

A chisel to test ice thickness

An ice augur

A short jigging rod designed for ice fishing, and a fixed-spool reel loaded with 10 lb (4.5 kg) breaking-strain line

A selection of ice-jigging lures

A friend to fish with (for safety)

**1** First, make absolutely sure that the ice is safe to walk on, following the ice safety checklist on the opposite page with an adult.

**2** After checking the ice, carefully make your way to the part of the frozen lake's surface you would like to fish on. Use your hand augur to drill a hole in the ice (get an adult to help you).

**3** Tie an ice jig (a kind of flashy lure that attracts predatory fish) to your line with a blood-knot. Lower it through the hole and let the line pay out until the line goes slack when the jig is resting on the bottom.

**4** Reel the lure up off the bottom by a couple of feet, then begin jigging the rod, rhythmically raising and lowering it to make the lure move attractively.

**5** After a couple of minutes, reel the lure up by another couple of feet and begin jigging again.

**6** When the lure reaches the surface, lower the lure to the bottom again and repeat the process.

**7** If you get a bite, give the rod a firm upward jerk to set the hook and carefully reel the fish to the surface. Take your time and allow the fish to tire naturally before attempting to land it.

**8** If you do not intend on eating the fish, remove the hook carefully with forceps and return it to the water. If you do intend on eating the fish, kill it humanely by striking it sharply on the head with a rounded rock or a short club called a "priest" (available from fishing stores).

## ICE SAFETY

When you're on ice you have to take extra special care and safety precautions. Never go onto the ice on your own, make sure an adult is with you, always wear a flotation device, and carry a safety line to throw to anyone who has fallen through the ice. Before venturing onto the ice, you should check for certain signs to make sure it is safe and thick enough to support your weight: do not go onto ice if it has melted away from the shore—this is a sign it is thawing. Ice thickness can vary, so test its depth with a chisel as you go along. Any ice less than 6 inches (15 cm) thick is potentially dangerous for a pair of people to walk on. Be very careful near shore, where variation in thickness is greatest. Do not venture onto ice near river mouths, bridges, or anywhere where swift currents run, as these reduce the thickness of ice. Ice near areas of open water should also be avoided. Safety should always come first.

# MAKING A SNOW ANGEL

Just as your feet leave prints in the snow when you walk, you can use other parts of your body to make fun shapes in the snow. You will have to lie down on the ground to make your snow angel, so make sure you are wearing warm, waterproof clothing before you start.

| SKILL LEVEL | ❄ |
| TIME NEEDED | One minute |

**YOU WILL NEED**

Fresh, newly fallen snow

Warm, waterproof clothing

**1** Find a patch of fresh, fluffy snow that is at least 3 inches (7.6 cm) deep.

**2** Lie down on your back on the patch of snow. Spread your arms out wide on either side, but keep your legs together.

**3** Move your arms up and down once or twice, like a bird flapping its wings. Then spread your legs out in a V-shape and bring them together again. Stand up to admire your handiwork.

# SNOW PAINTING

This activity is fun, messy, and bright, but you will need a few basic items of equipment. First, you'll need to obtain three pump-action sprayers—the kind used to water household plants. Ask permission to use any you may already have at home, and make sure they're thoroughly rinsed out before use. Or, new sprayers can be obtained fairly cheaply from hardware stores. You'll also need some food dyes. Green, red, and blue are a good basic set of colors. Mixed with water, these will form the "paints" that you will apply to the snow using the sprayers.

| | |
|---|---|
| SKILL LEVEL | ❄ ❄ |
| TIME NEEDED | 40 minutes |

**1** Fill each sprayer with water and add a small amount of a different food dye to each. Replace the top and give it a little shake to mix the color with the water properly.

**2** Find a clean patch of snow outside and, carefully aiming the nozzle of the sprayer, paint lines onto the snow by squirting on color. Use the other colors you have chosen to build up a picture.

**3** Using this technique, you can make simple pictures of anything from flowers to faces. You can even paint details onto a snowman (see page 46) or snow sculptures (see page 63).

## YOU WILL NEED

Three pump-action sprayers

Water

Food dyes

Snow

## TOP TIPS

When buying your spray bottles, try to get clear ones so that you can see what color your snow paint is inside. Label the spray bottles using a permanent marker with whatever color is in each bottle. They will keep for at least a year stored in the fridge.

Don't completely fill the bottle with water. Leave at least an inch (2.5 cm) of the bottle empty so that you can add the food coloring and still be able to put on the spray nozzle.

# ADVENTURE PLAYGROUND

It doesn't always snow in winter, but there's still plenty of fun to be had outside. Building an adventure playground in your own backyard will give you an exciting base for all-day-long fun. Here are some suggestions for some features that should be reasonably easy to construct at home.

**SKILL LEVEL** ❄ ❄ ❄
**TIME NEEDED** One day

**TIRE SWING** Obtain a worn-out car tire (ask at your local junkyard if you don't have any at hand), and a length of strong rope. Ask an adult to tie the rope securely to a low branch of an overhanging tree that's strong enough to support the weight of a full-grown person, and then secure the other end to your tire so that it hangs at about waist height. Make sure there's plenty of room on either side for the swing to work in, and soft turf or woodchips beneath.

**GROUND LOOPS** Larger tires can make another playground feature. Obtain a tractor tire from a junkyard and, with help from an adult, dig a hole in the ground deep enough to hold slightly more than half the tire when it is standing upright. Place the tire in the hole and fill in any gaps with earth up to ground height. Pack down any rough surfaces with loose soil. You can now use the tire to climb on and crawl through. If you have the time—and enough tires— place three tires side by side to make a tunnel or ridge of tires that you can clamber through or hop across.

**SANDBOX** A sandbox is a classic play accessory. First, work out how large you want the sandbox to be. Then go to a hardware store and buy enough 1- inch- (2.5 cm-) thick, weather-treated hardwood planks to make the sides of the box. Excavate the desired area of soil to the same depth as the planks are wide. Cut the planks to length with a handsaw and fit them in position, upright on their sides, pegging them in place with thick pegs of wood driven into the soil so they hold the planks in position. Then fill the box up to the brim with builder's sand.

## YOU WILL NEED

Worn-out tires

A strong rope

An overhanging tree

Tractor tires

A shovel

Some 1-in-(2.5-cm-) thick weather-treated planks

A handsaw

Some thick wood pegs

Sand

Adult assistance

# MAKING A SLED

With a fresh fall of snow, you'll want to ride the powder like an Arctic explorer, so you will need a sled. Nothing gets you from A to B faster when the ground is thick with snow. And, if it doesn't snow where you are—or you want to use your sled in summer—you can still slide on a flat-bottomed sled down smooth, grassy, or sandy slopes.  If you weren't in time to beat the rush on sleds at the first snowfall, you can build your own. This is an advanced project, so you'll need some help from your family, especially an adult to help with the sawing and drilling, or some friends and a few tools. You might even need a trip to the hardware store—if you're not snowed in! You can cut all the wood you need from a single large sheet of plywood.

| | |
|---|---|
| **SKILL LEVEL** | ❊ ❊ ❊ |
| **TIME NEEDED** | 2 days |

## YOU WILL NEED

A 2- x 4-ft- (0.6- x 1.2-m-), 1-in- (2.5-cm-) thick sheet of plywood (top board)

A saw

Some sandpaper

A 1-in- (2.5-cm-) wide chisel or router with 1-in- (2.5-cm-) bit

Two 1- x 4-ft (0.3- x 1.2-m), 1-in- (2.5-cm-) thick plywood (runners)

Wood glue

At least eight 2-in (5-cm) screws

A screwdriver

Four angle irons 6 in (15 cm) on each side, with at least four ¼-in- (0.5-cm-) wide bolt holes

A pencil

Drill with a ¼-in (0.5-cm) bit

At least 1½-in- (3.8-cm-) long, ¼-in (0.5-cm-) wide bolts with plenty of washers and nuts

2 ft (0.5 m) of rope

**1** Take the top board and cut off the corners of one end with a saw. Round off the corners where you've cut with sandpaper to make a semicircle which will be the front of your sled.

**2** Use sandpaper to round off the back corners of the top board while you're there—rounded corners make falling off less painful.

**3** Use a chisel or router to create two 1-inch- (2.5-cm-) wide, ¼-inch- (0.5-cm-) deep grooves along the length of the top board, about 1 ½ inch (3 cm) in from the sides. The two runners for your sled will fit into these grooves.

**4** Stack the two runners on top of each other and cut off the top right and bottom left corners.

**5** Sand the cut corners on both runners to make a smooth curve. This will run along the snow.

**6** Place a thread of wood glue along the top edge of each runner and then fit them into the grooves on the top board.

**7** Secure the runners in place by drilling screws down into them through the top board.

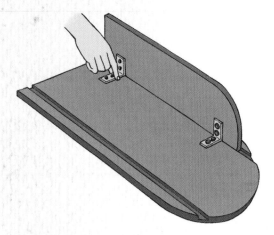

**8** Turn the sled upside down and lay the angle irons—iron strips bent at a right angle—in the corner between the runner and the bottom of the sled. Use two angle irons for each runner, placing one at the front and one at the back. Use a pencil to mark the location of the bolt holes.

**9** Remove the angle irons and drill holes all the way through the top board and runners where you have marked.

**10** Secure the angle irons in place with bolts to hold the runners securely in place. Use washers on both sides of the board.

**11** Drill a hole in the very front of your sled, and loop the rope through it so you've got something to hold onto.

**12** Your sled is ready to go. You can decorate your sled with paint, or any other embellishments you like. Then all you need to do is wait for a good snowfall to try it out. Start off on gentle slopes to get the hang of sledding, and keep an eye out for fences, other sledders, and any other potential obstacles in your path.

### TOP TIP

For a sturdier structure, take your finished sled to a blacksmith and have metal runners fitted over the wooden ones—that'll protect them from unexpected rocks lurking beneath the snow. You can also coat the whole structure in waterproof lacquer or polyurethane to keep water out of the wood and stop it from rotting.

# CATCHING SNOWFLAKES

Although thousands of snowflakes can fall every minute, no two are ever alike. Next time it snows, catch a couple of flakes so that you can examine the unique, beautiful, and complex ice crystals of each one.

| SKILL LEVEL | ❄ |
|---|---|
| TIME NEEDED | 5 minutes |

## YOU WILL NEED

Falling snow

Black craft card

A magnifying glass

Pencil and paper

**1** Take a sheet of stiff black card outside when it is snowing, and hold it out flat in front of you.

**2** In a few moments, flakes of snow will gather on it, showing up clear and white on the black background. Use a magnifying glass to view them up close.

**3** Try to remember how each one looks. Then, when you go inside, make pencil drawings of what you saw, so you'll have a record of these fragile wonders that lasts long after the snowflakes have melted forever.

# ICE ART

When ponds and lakes freeze over, leaves and other things are trapped in a layer of crystal-clear ice. Replicate this fascinating process by making an amazing ice mobile.

| SKILL LEVEL | ❄ ❄ |
|---|---|
| TIME NEEDED | 24 hours |

## YOU WILL NEED

3 shallow plastic tubs

A tray

Some garden twine or wood

1 liter of water

Some natural objects

**1** Find three shallow plastic tubs and place them on a tray. Lay a length of garden twine or wool across all three, so it rests flat on the bottom of each dish, with a little slack twine between them.

**2** Place a natural object, such as a feather or plant frond, in each dish, across the twine on the bottom, and then carefully fill each dish with water.

**3** If it's freezing conditions outside, leave the tray out overnight, or place it in the freezer.

**4** In the morning, the water in the tubs will have frozen—encasing your natural artifacts in ice. Remove the ice mobile from the tubs and hang it up outside from the twine that links it together.

# ICE SKATING

Learning how to skate can be hard (and so can the ice when you fall on it). But once you get the hang of it, you can set up goals, get some sticks and a puck, and play hockey. If you really want to show off, you can even skate backwards! Knowing how to skate starts with a snugly fitting pair of ice skates. The general rule of thumb is to pick a skate about half a size smaller than your normal shoe size. Lace them up tight enough so that your ankles won't turn in, but not so tight that you cut off circulation to your feet.

| SKILL LEVEL | ❄ ❄ ❄ |
| --- | --- |
| TIME NEEDED | 1–2 hours |

## YOU WILL NEED

A frozen pond, river, lake, or rink

A pair of ice skates

Warm clothing

## BEGINNER STEPS

**1** To stabilize yourself right away, use little side steps to work your way out onto the ice.

**2** Find your balance by keeping your feet slightly apart, with your knees bent and your arms extended in front of you. Bend slightly at the waist to keep your weight balanced front to back.

**3** Keeping this position, point your toes slightly inward until your feet come together. Then push your skates out until they glide out to shoulder width before pointing your toes inward again to bring your skates back together.

**4** Repeat these motions and you should glide across the ice! This type of skating is called "sculling."

### WARNING

It is almost impossible to judge the thickness of the ice on frozen lakes and ponds, so you should never go skating outdoors on the ice without permission or someone in attendance.

Falling on hard ice really hurts. If you think you're going to fall, bend your knees and try to slide down on your side rather than put your hands down.

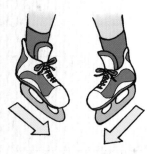

## INTERMEDIATE STEPS

**1** Once you have a feel for the ice, you can graduate to the more advanced left-right-left skating style. This will let you move faster and more smoothly.

**2** Start by bending your knees and leaning on your left foot while pushing out and back on the ice with your right skate. You should start gliding forward on your left skate.

**3** Next, bend your knees and lean on your right foot and push out and back on the ice with your left skate.

**4** Repeat the process and you should start to glide smoothly across the ice!

**5** As you gain confidence, push a little harder with your back foot to move yourself along a little faster.

**6** Stop your forward momentum by holding one skate blade horizontally behind you.

## SKATING BACKWARDS

**1** Start with your head up, knees bent, and back straight—the same position for the beginner steps.

**2** The idea is to "scull" in the opposite direction, so point your heels in until your feet come together, then push them out to shoulder width. Getting someone to give you a gentle backward push can help you get started.

**3** Repeat the motions as you did for sculling forward: bring your heels together, then push your skates out, then bring them together again. Remember to keep an eye out behind you!

**4** Always keep your knees bent, and don't bend your waist forward or you could lose your balance.

**5** When you're feeling truly confident, you can try turning around as you skate, so you switch from going forward to gliding backwards. This takes some practice, so be prepared for a few bruises before you get it right.

### FRICTION

Ever wondered why you can skate on a sheet of ice but not, say, on a concrete pavement? It's because of friction—the force that makes it hard to slide two surfaces against each other. Ice creates much less friction with other surfaces than concrete does—that's why when you walk on ice, you slip. There is still some—without friction, you'd simply step on the ice and keep going in that direction until you ran into the wall on the other side of the rink. When you're skating, the thin blade of steel, rather than the bottom of your sneakers, has less surface to rub against so you'll have even less friction. In fact, the blade creates enough pressure under your weight to melt the ice slightly, creating a thin layer of water that reduces the friction even further. So you see, skates are actually pretty clever inventions!

# SPINNING

**1** Spinning is the best part of figure skating for both boys and girls—it looks fantastic and impressive, but don't attempt this until you're confident at gliding around the rink. The first spin to learn is the two-foot spin, where you keep both blades in contact with the ice. You can spin either to the right or to the left, whichever feels most natural for you.

**2** Start with your feet about hip distance apart. Stand with your back straight, your chin raised, and your arms curved at chest height in front of you to form a loose circle. Now place the right toepick (front tip of the blade) into the ice.

**3** Next, bring your left arm around in front of you and your right arm back behind you, with the palms facing down. Let your left foot follow around as you move your arms.

**4** As you bring your arms briskly back to the front, in rounded circle position, keeping your feet still at hip width apart, you should start to turn. Allow yourself to turn through a whole revolution.

**5** If you remember to keep looking up, you may even get two turns or more from this move (looking down slows the spin and makes you feel dizzy).

**6** Keep practicing, and if you find that you're moving across the ice rather than staying in one spot, then try turning your right foot in slightly as this can help to keep the spin centered. If you want to look and feel like a real figure skater, then you must make sure your posture is good: shoulders down, back straight, and chin up. Ta da—a real star in the making!

## DID YOU KNOW?

Before ice skating became a cold-weather leisure sport, early humans in modern-day Europe and Russia used animal bones strapped to their feet to make it easier to travel across frozen terrain. The Dutch are credited with inventing the metal blades we're all familiar with. The design was first seen in paintings from about 800 years ago and it hasn't changed much since.

# WINTER GAMES

In cold weather, the best way to keep warm outdoors is by running around in the fresh, crisp air. You may not be able to build a full-size stadium in your backyard, but there's no reason you can't hold your own thrilling winter games event. The main thing is to plan races that will put a variety of athletic skills to the test, from speed to balance to agility. Like all contests, winter games are most fun when you have a good number of competitors and events. You might want to offer some prizes for the winners as an extra incentive, such as a bag of candy or maybe medals made of chocolate coins. Once you have assembled your competitors and prepared everything you need, it's time to let the games begin—and may the best person win!

| SKILL LEVEL | ❄ ❄ |
| --- | --- |
| TIME NEEDED | 3 hours |

## DRESSING-UP RACE

Polar explorers need to put on a lot of warm clothing and equipment before they can venture out onto the tundra (which is like a desert that has ice instead of sand). This race tests the ability of competitors to dress up in full gear in a hurry! It will also get everyone warmed up nicely for the other events.

**YOU WILL NEED**

**A variety of winter clothing**

**1** Before the race, prepare a bag of bulky outdoor clothing and items for each competitor—you can include things like parka jackets, waterproof pants, snow goggles, a furry hat, snowshoes, and a backpack: in fact, the more the better—as long as each bag contains similar items. For extra entertainment value, try placing in a few silly items like pink fluffy earmuffs!

**2** Place the bags in a row about 65 feet (20 meters) from the start line.

**3** The aim is to see who can get all of the items on first, so when the judge blows a whistle, the competitors must race each other to their bags.

**4** The first one to don all their items and shout "Ready!" is the winner.

# GOLD RUSH RELAY

**1** This race is a test of co-operation and teamwork. First, ask competitors to form pairs. Each pair must stand back-to-back at the start line and link arms with their partner.

**2** Beside each pair, place a chair with three tennis balls on it. These are the nuggets of "gold."

**3** Without unlinking arms, pairs must stoop so one of the pair can pick up one of the nuggets.

**4** They must then make their way to a bucket placed 33 feet (10 meters) away. This is the "bank," and the aim of the game is to be the first pair to pick up and drop all three of their gold nuggets in the bank without unlinking arms or dropping their cargo. If any drop their gold, they must return to the start line and begin that run again.

**YOU WILL NEED**

Chairs

Tennis balls

A large plastic tub/bucket

# ICEBERG BALANCE

**1** Find two strong but low boxes—such as empty bottle crates—and set them upside down, about 6.5 feet (2 meters) apart, on soft ground or snow. These will be the "icebergs."

**2** Next, select two competitors and have them each stand on a box. Take a length of rope and hand one end to each competitor.

**3** The aim of the game is to tug the other person off their iceberg, but watch out—there's more than one way to win. Quick, unexpected tugs, or alternatively, letting the rope slip through your fingers at the right moment, can catch a ham-fisted opponent off balance and win you the match more surely than pure strength alone.

**YOU WILL NEED**

Two boxes

Some rope

## ICE FISHING RACE

**1** Buy or borrow 50 to 100 ping-pong balls (online auction sites often sell them in bulk for cheap).

**2** Next, fill a large plastic tub with water and empty the balls into it—these are the "fish." You can throw in a few ice cubes, too, if you want to really set the scene.

**3** Give each competitor a small handheld fishing net of the kind used at the ocean to catch crabs.

**4** When the judge blows a whistle, each competitor must try to scoop as many fish into their net as possible and carry them to their own bucket ten paces behind the tub.

**5** The game ends when all the "fish" have been collected. The winner is the one who has the biggest catch in his or her bucket.

**YOU WILL NEED**

50–100 ping-pong balls

A large plastic tub

Small handheld fishing nets

## SLED RACES

**1** Competitors must bring their own sleds, but may customize them for speed as much as they like.

**2** Before the contest begins, mark a finish line at the bottom of the slope, using traffic cones or similarly robust but safe markers. You can stretch tape between them for a proper race-day feel if you wish.

**3** When the judge's whistle blows, the first sled to cross the line wins.

**4** If you have a lot of competitors (say, more than twelve), run races of three sleds, with the winner of each race going through to race the winners of the other races in a grand, final run.

**5** Alternatively, you can stage the race as a time-trial event, with the fastest overall time from start to finish taking victory—competitors take turns one after the other, and everyone gets three attempts at making a record-breaking run.

**YOU WILL NEED**

A sled for each player

Two traffic cones

A stopwatch

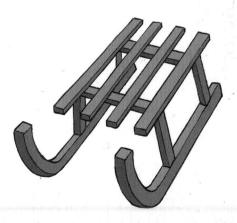

# SCAVENGER HUNT

The aim of a classic scavenger hunt is to find as many items as you can from a list of objects drawn up at the start of the game. To add an up-to-date twist, players may also photograph some of the objects on the list instead of physically retrieving them. This means you can include large or living things like snowmen or trees in the hunt. Each of the items on the list should have a score associated with it that corresponds to how easy or hard it is to find. For example, objects that are simple to find might score only one point, whereas something a bit more difficult might score two. Try to keep the scoring system fairly simple, otherwise it'll be tricky to total up scores at the end.

| | |
|---|---|
| **SKILL LEVEL** | ❄ ❄ |
| **TIME NEEDED** | 2 hours or more |

**1** Make a list of items to for the scavengers to find—twenty or so should be fine. Try to choose objects that are associated with winter and the holiday season. Assign a score to each object on the list and decide which items players need to physically retrieve and which they must photograph instead (larger items). Print or write out copies of the list to give to players.

**2** Decide an area in which to play the game. For example, you could hold the game inside your own house or widen the permitted search area to include friends' houses and yards, too.

**3** Set a time limit for the game depending on how many objects there are. The shorter the game, the more fast and furious the hunt will be.

**4** Assemble the competitors— you can play as individuals or teams. Make sure everyone knows the rules and has a list of the items that must be found. Remind players to politely ask permission to borrow objects on the list that don't belong to them.

**5** When the game is over, each player or team must present their finds so their total score can be added up. The winner, or winners, get a round of applause, or a prize.

## YOU WILL NEED

A list of items for players to find

Two or more players

A camera for each player or team

A pen and paper to total up scores at the end

## DID YOU KNOW?

Every year, a giant scavenger hunt called the Tricadecathlonomania (try saying that quickly) takes place. Although the idea originated in Northfield, Minnesota, teams from around the world now take part in this huge 24-hour event.

# GATHERING GREENERY

Many trees lose all their leaves in the fall. After a brief blaze of red and gold, they stand bare as broomsticks until warmer weather brings new buds to the branches in spring. Some trees, known as evergreens, keep their leaves all year round. Evergreens often have waxy, needle-shaped leaves that help the tree to conserve water—which is why they can survive on freezing, stoney mountain slopes high above green valleys below. Make a wreath of winter greenery to hang on your front door as a reminder that life continues to flourish even in the darkest part of the year.

**SKILL LEVEL**  ❄ ❄

**TIME NEEDED**  1 hour

**1** Obtain an inexpensive willow, vine or straw wreath form from a florist. This will be the frame on which you will construct your wreath of winter greenery.

**2** Gather some slender, supple fronds from the tips of the branches of evergreen trees. Cedar, firs, pines, holly, and juniper branches can all be used. Remove them carefully with pruning shears. Never remove greenery from a conservation or protected area.

**3** Trim the evergreen fronds into small lengths of 6 inches (15 cm) or so.

**4** Lay the wreath form on a table. Then begin attaching the fronds to the form by pushing the ends of the fronds into the twiggy structure of the wreath form, twisting the fronds around it where necessary.

**5** Add more fronds all around the wreath form, until it forms a dense and bushy ring of greenery. Use florist's wire to secure any stray fronds.

**6** Add decorations such as winter berries (make sure they're non-toxic), ribbons, bows, or mock presents, binding them on with florist's wire here and there.

## YOU WILL NEED

**A wreath form**

**Some evergreen fronds**

**A pair of pruning shears**

**Florist's wire**

**Any extra decorative items you want**

## TOP TIP

If you do not have any winter greenery at hand, ask politely at a Christmas tree wholesaler and they will usually give you any broken or discarded branches they wish to dispose of.

# BUILDING AN IGLOO

Igloos are buildings made out of snow blocks. They are the traditional homes for the Inuit people of Canada and Alaska. Some people might think the Inuit build with ice and snow because they like to be cold, but in fact, snow has very good insulating qualities because it holds a lot of air. That means when the air outside an igloo is -40°F (-40°C), the inside of an igloo can be a toasty 60°F (16°C), even without a fire. The warmth inside an igloo comes from body heat. Building an igloo is surprisingly easy to do. You just need to have the right kind of snow and lots of it. When an igloo is built correctly, a fully grown man can stand on top of the dome without it caving in. The Inuit bring a small lamp inside their igloos to melt the inside of the walls slightly and make them turn into ice to help reinforce the strength of the dome. Whenever you're sitting on cold ground or snow, your body temperature is going to drop because the ground draws the heat away. Try to sit on a raised platform or chair to stay warm inside your igloo.

| SKILL LEVEL | ❄ ❄ ❄ |
|---|---|
| TIME NEEDED | 2-3 hours |

## YOU WILL NEED

A snow shovel

A pair of waterproof, insulated gloves

Lots of dry, very hard snow

A snow saw

**1** Find a large supply of dry, hard snow—you want unbroken ice crystals in the snow if possible.

**2** Cut blocks from the snow. Get an adult to help you. Each block should be 3 feet (90 cm) long, 15 inches (40 cm) high, and 8 inches (20 cm) deep.

**3** As you cut the blocks, begin arranging them in an upwards-sloping spiral around yourself. You will be working from the inside of the dome. Shape the first block so that it slants upwards, and work your way around. The hole you're making as you cut the blocks will become the floor of the igloo. Make the initial circle 6 feet (2 m) in diameter.

**4** As you build the walls up, shape each block with your snow saw so that they all slant slightly upwards and lean slightly inwards to form a dome shape. Don't worry about the front door just yet.

## DID YOU KNOW?

Although you might think all igloos are made from snow, the big ones often have a tent inside. Snow is a very good insulator, so piling it around the outsides of your tent actually helps to keep heat in!

**5** When you get near the top and there isn't any more room to stack blocks, cut a hole at ground level for the front door. It should be no more than 2 feet (60 cm) high.

**6** Close off the top of the igloo by cutting a block of snow in the shape of the hole. Make it slightly larger than the hole. Place it on top of the igloo, then go inside and use your snow saw to cut and shape the top block so that it drops snugly into the hole.

**7** Cut four more blocks and lean them teepee-fashion over the entrance tunnel. This tunnel will keep wind and snow out of the igloo and will also help funnel cold air out of the igloo.

**8** Go back inside the igloo and cut two 3-inch (8-cm) ventilation holes in opposite sides of the igloo dome at about waist height. This also allows cold air to escape, while the warm air gets trapped under the dome.

## IGLOO VARIATIONS

If you live in an area with warm winters, you can still make your own igloo. Some people have successfully built sand igloos at the beach, but that's an inexact science where luck plays as much of a role as the building material—you need the right mix of sand and water.

If you live in the desert, you can try mud brick igloos. The Native Americans used to create bricks out of caliche, a fine dirt found in the southwest United States. They would make a mix of mud, straw, and water, pack it into brick-sized wooden molds, and bake them in the sun for a few days.

If you can't get ahold of sand or caliche, there's always a papier mâché igloo. Make an igloo shape out of chicken wire and cover it in strips of newspaper soaked in paste made from flour and water. With a bit of white paint and a little imagination, this can make quite a cozy igloo substitute for the summer months. And unlike the snow igloo, this version will never melt—until it rains!

### WARNING

Although it will be warmer inside the igloo than outside, you will still need to wear warm clothing and use a winter sleeping bag if you want to spend the night without getting cold!

# MAKING AN ICICLE

Icicles can sometimes be seen hanging from the roofs of buildings in very cold climates. Icicles form in cold weather when dripping water freezes into a long, clear spindle of ice. If you want to view this fascinating natural phenomenon up close, you can try making your own. All you need to do is make a container that slowly drips water—then hang it outside on a particularly cold night.

| SKILL LEVEL | ❄ ❄ |
|---|---|
| TIME NEEDED | ½ hour |

**1** First, find a suitable container. An old coffee tin is perfect.

**2** Using a bradawl, carefully make two holes, one facing the other on either side of the tin, two centimeters or so below its top rim. Ask an adult for help if you find this part difficult.

**3** Thread the string through both holes and then tie the ends of the string together securely to form a loop from which to hang the tin.

**4** Next, take a thumbtack and carefully puncture a small hole in the base of the tin. It should be just big enough to allow water to gradually drip out.

**5** Wait until a freezing night is forecast. Then fill your container with water and hang it outside at dusk. If there isn't a convenient nail on a wall to hang it from, try a low branch in the yard.

**6** Visit it in the morning—a beautiful icicle should have formed beneath the tin. For a splash of extra fun, try adding food coloring to the water before hanging up the tin. With practice, you'll be able to make icicles of all colors of the rainbow.

## YOU WILL NEED

**An empty coffee tin**

**A bradawl**

**A 28-in (70-cm) piece of string**

**A thumbtack**

**A tape measure**

**A pair of scissors**

**Water**

**Food dye (optional)**

### DID YOU KNOW?

In the right conditions, natural icicles can grow to more than 20 feet (6 m) in length.

# SNOW SCULPTURES

Snow seems almost purpose-made for people to have fun with. It is soft enough to mold into different forms but holds its shape when packed firm. This means you can use it to make amazing sculptures that will adorn your yard until the weather thaws. A snowman (see page 46) is one of the simplest kinds of snow sculptures. But, although snowmen are as much a part of winter as rosy cheeks, you needn't feel limited to this familiar design. Animals, castles, and mountains are almost as easy to make, and it doesn't stop there.

**SKILL LEVEL** ❄ ❄ ❄

**TIME NEEDED** 1–3 hours

## YOU WILL NEED

Plenty of fallen snow

Warm outdoor clothing and gloves

A garden shovel

A garden trowel

Plastic tubs of different shapes and sizes

A pump-action spray bottle

Water

Food dye (optional)

**1** Wait for a day when thick drifts of snow lie on the ground.

**2** Using a garden shovel, make a big heap of snow. This will be the basic resource from which you make the sculpture.

**3** Decide what you want to make, then shape the snow into a rough outline. Use the shovel to carve out big shapes and a garden trowel to form smaller shapes, patting the snow down firm as you go.

**4** Household objects like plastic tubs can help you mold snow into useful shapes that can be added to the design, such as blocks or columns. You can also roll snow into balls that can form the basic segments of a bigger design, such as a caterpillar. Always be careful not to build anything that might collapse on top of someone and hurt them, though.

**5** Once you have built your basic design, use a pump-action spray bottle to spray it with water. This will form a thin film of ice on the surface that will allow you to carve out fine details with a spoon. Alternatively, use food dye to add splashes of color to your piece of frozen art.

# LEARNING TO SKI

There is no sensation quite like skiing. Gliding fast on skis over crisp snow is as near to the sensation of flying as you can get without sprouting wings. Although skiing is a sport that requires special equipment, it's best to rent the essentials to start with while you decide if you like the sport. When you first start, look for "bunny slopes"—miniature slopes for beginners to practice on. It's best to have a professional instructor to guide you, but here are some of the basic moves:

| SKILL LEVEL | ❄ ❄ ❄ |
|---|---|
| TIME NEEDED | 1 day |

## YOU WILL NEED

A pair of skis

A pair of ski boots

A set of ski poles

A pair of ski goggles

Warm, waterproof clothes

Access to a bunny slope

**GETTING USED TO SKIS** Before you start your downhill run, it's best to get a feel for the basic moves that will help you balance and steer when you begin your descent. Standing on a flat surface, bend your knees slightly then lift one ski slightly off the ground. Place it back on the ground and lift the other. Try raising the tip and tail of each ski and also tilting them so the tips meet together in a "snowplow" (see "the stance" below).

**WALKING IN SKIS** Walking in skis is an essential skill to master. It will enable you to position yourself properly at the top of the slope before you begin your downhill run and to move out of the way of other skiers once you have reached the bottom. Walking in skis is like normal walking, except you do not lift your feet off the floor. Instead, you slide the skis forward one after the other, swinging your arms as you would do normally.

**THE STANCE** Before you start to ski, you'll need to adopt a stance that will allow you to remain stable and upright when in motion. The best posture for beginners is the snowplow stance. This allows you to glide slowly down the slope under full control. First, bend your knees slightly and position your hands—holding the ski poles—just above your thighs. Then angle the tips of your skis toward one another so they form an arrowhead shape, with the tails of the skis splayed wide apart behind you. Practice this stance before you try moving downhill.

# SKIING MOVES AND TECHNIQUES

The below instructions cover the first steps, but the best way to begin is by taking lessons from a professional instructor who will be able to guide you every step of the way and help you learn from your mistakes as you become more confident and adept on the slopes.

**1** When you're ready to start, position yourself at the top of the bunny slope in the snowplow stance. Lean forward slightly and you should start moving gently downhill, aided by gravity alone.

**2** If at any point you wish to slow down or stop, simply increase the wedge-shaped angle of your skis when in the snowplow stance, so the tips are closer together and the tails are splayed wider apart. This should bring you to a halt.

**3** Once you are moving forward at a gentle pace, try some shallow turns—place your weight on the ski opposite to the direction you wish to turn in. Once you have gained confidence, you can trace a zig-zag path down the slope, looking all around you to make sure you are not moving into the path of another skier.

**4** If you do fall, don't worry. It's normal to have a few falls when learning, and the snow will cushion your landing. To get up, position yourself on your side with your skis parallel to one another, one slightly lower than the other. The skis should be aligned so they are at right angles to the slope—preventing you from sliding down as you get up. Then, place your ski poles together and dig their tips into the snow beside you. Lever yourself into an upright position, using the poles for support.

**5** To move uphill, use side steps. Position your skis so they are at right angles to the slope, then shift your weight slightly onto the downhill ski. As you do so, lift your uphill ski off the ground and move it sideways a few inches higher up the slope. Once it is in place, move your weight onto the uphill ski and move the downhill ski upwards in the same way. Steady yourself with your ski poles if necessary. Reverse the process to step downhill.

## DID YOU KNOW?

The fastest professional downhill skiers can reach speeds well in excess of 100 mph on special high-altitude courses where air-resistance is lower. The world record is held by Italian Simone Origone, who was clocked traveling at 156.2 mph on a French course in 2006.

## TOP TIP

Ski store staff will help you find the best-sized skis for you, but a rough rule of thumb is that you should choose skis that, when stood on their ends, reach up to your eye level.

# INDOOR PLAY

When the frost bites hard, or grey, sleet-heavy clouds block out the crisp winter sunshine, it's time to start a fire and invite friends inside for games, stories, and other classic forms of indoor entertainment. You can test out your competitive streak with a good old-fashioned card game. Or, why not play the party favorite game of charades or conduct some fun science experiments. Whatever you're in the mood for, you will find the perfect activity for a cold winter's afternoon here.

# PLAYING CARD GAMES

Sometimes you just need to be able to kill some time, and that's where card games come in, especially on a cold, wintery day, spending hours indoors. Most card games are good for any number of players, don't need a lot of time to prepare, and require only a pack of cards, making them ideal for afternoons stuck inside waiting for the weather to improve.

| SKILL LEVEL | ❄ ❄ |
| --- | --- |
| TIME REQUIRED | 1–2 hours |

## GERMAN WHIST

**1** Each person is dealt a hand of 13 cards. The remaining cards are left in a pile on the table between you, facedown but with the top card turned over (faceup) on top of the deck. The suit of this faceup card becomes the trump suit for the game. This is explained a little later.

**2** In the first stage of this game, you are trying to get good (i.e., high-value) cards from the pile to improve your hand. The non-dealer goes first. He can play any card in his hand and the other player must play a card of the same suit if possible. If the other player has no cards in the suit that was led, she can play any card.

**3** If both cards are the same suit, the higher card wins the trick— so a nine beats a seven, a king beats a jack, and an ace beats any other card in that suit. If the cards are of different suits, the first player wins unless the second player has a trump

card, in which case the trump wins. If two trumps are played, the higher card wins.

**4** When you win a trick, you take the face-up card on top of the pile and add it to your hand. The loser takes the next card from the pile (facedown) without showing her opponent and adds it to her hand so that both players again have 13 cards. The two cards that were used in the trick are turned facedown and set aside. The top card on the remaining pile is then turned faceup and the winner of the last trick leads the next card.

**5** Continue playing in this way until there are no cards left in the center pile.

**6** Once the pile has been used up, with the cards in your hand, you continue to play (the winner of the last trick of the first stage leads), this time without replenishing

### YOU WILL NEED

A standard deck of 52 playing cards (jokers removed)

Another player

your hands. Now the aim is to win as many tricks as possible. You place your won tricks facedown in front of you, and whoever has the most tricks at the end of this stage wins the game.

**7** Did you notice how the tricks won in the first stage do not help you to win the second stage? Actually, all you want to do in the first stage is to collect cards in your hand that will enable you to win the most tricks in the second stage. So don't try to win an exposed card on the top of the pile if it's not very good or unless it's likely to be better than the unseen card beneath it. For example, if diamonds are trumps and the exposed card is a four of hearts, you should definitely try to lose this trick by laying one of your poorer cards. Make sense? Don't worry, it will all become clear when you start to play.

# GO FISH

**1** If only two people are playing, deal seven cards to each person. For more than two players, deal out five cards each. Keep the rest of the cards together and place them in the middle of the table.

**2** The youngest player starts by asking one other person in the game for a card number to match a card in his or her hand. For example, if you have a two of hearts in your hand, you ask one other player if they have any twos.

**3** If they do, they must hand one to you. When you get a pair, you lay the pair down in front of you faceup and ask again.

**4** When you ask for a card and the person you ask does not have it, they say "Go fish." This means you draw one card off the top of the deck. If the card you draw matches a card in your hand, you lay the pair down and ask again. If it does not match any other card in your hand, you keep the card you've picked, but your turn is over and the person on your left gets a turn to ask.

**5** The game is played until all the cards in the deck have been drawn and all the pairs have been matched. The person with the most pairs wins.

## YOU WILL NEED

**A standard deck of 52 playing cards (jokers removed)**

**One to nine other players**

# PARACHUTE GAMES

Don't worry, this doesn't involve jumping out of an airplane! Parachute games are a test of teamwork and coordination that will keep a group of friends in high spirits on a winter afternoon. As a genuine parachute will probably be difficult to obtain, a large, lightweight sheet of fabric makes a good substitute, and the larger and lighter it is, the better.

| | |
|---|---|
| SKILL LEVEL | ❉ |
| TIME NEEDED | 40 minutes |

**1** Lay your parachute flat on the floor in a large room. Ask players to space themselves evenly around the edge of the fabric, facing inwards toward its center.

**2** When everyone is standing in position, ask the players to pick up the edge of the parachute in front of them with both hands. The parachute should now be held off the ground at about waist height by the ring of players. You're ready to begin.

**3** First, try a basic "mushroom." On a count of three, everybody must lift their arms above their heads (still holding onto the edge of the parachute), then lower them again. The fabric should billow up into a mushroom shape and then collapse downwards. To make things more interesting, place a beanbag in the middle of the parachute and see if you can flick it into the air with a rapid "mushroom" movement.

**4** Next, try a "Mexican wave." One after the other, in a clockwise sequence, each player must lift the edge of the parachute above their head, then lower it down quickly again. This will create a spectacular, circular ripple effect that will continue for as long as the players can keep it up.

**5** Finally, try playing "popcorn." For this, you'll need ten lightweight plastic balls in two colors (five green and five red, for example). Divide the players into two corresponding teams. To start the game, throw all the balls onto the parachute. By rapidly raising and lowering the fabric, the players must try to get all of the balls of their team's color to fly off the parachute and onto the floor. The first team to do so wins.

## YOU WILL NEED

A large, lightweight sheet of fabric

Open space

Eight or more players

Colored plastic balls

# PLAYING MARBLES

Contrary to what most kids might think, marbles isn't just a boring game your grandfather used to play. It actually takes skill and strategy. Marbles is a really old game—there are references to it in Roman literature from 2,000 years ago.

| | |
|---|---|
| **SKILL LEVEL** | ✳ ✳ |
| **TIME REQUIRED** | 1 hour |

**1** Use a stick to draw a 10-foot- (3-m-) diameter circle on the ground. This is going to be your playing area.

**2** To decide who goes first, each player stands on one edge of the circle and tries to flick their shooter as close as possible to the opposite side of the circle without going outside the line. The player whose marble lands closest to the line without crossing it wins the first shot.

**3** Once you've determined who shoots first, place the 13 smaller marbles in a cross pattern in the middle of the circle.

**4** The first player stands outside the circle and flicks his shooter at the marbles. Your knuckles should be aimed at the ground, but they cannot touch the ground. The goal of the game is to knock the smaller marbles out of the circle.

**5** When a player knocks out a smaller marble, he can take another turn and continue shooting until he fails to knock a smaller marble

out. After the first turn, you shoot from wherever your shooter landed inside the circle on the last shot. Keep any marbles you knock out of the ring to one side in your own pile–this is how you keep score.

**6** If you fail to knock a marble out, your opponent takes over and you cannot move your shooter from where it sits in the ring until he finishes his turn (by failing to knock any marbles out with one of his throws).

**7** Now your opponent can either try to knock out the small marbles, or try to knock your shooter out of the ring. If he succeeds in knocking out your shooter, then he gets to keep all the marbles you've gathered, and you lose the game.

**8** You can win by either knocking your opponent's shooter out of the ring, or by having more marbles than your opponent when all the small ones have been knocked out.

## YOU WILL NEED

**Two players**

**Thirteen small marbles**

**Two big marbles, called the "shooters"**

**A flat, open patch of ground at least 10 ft (3 m) around**

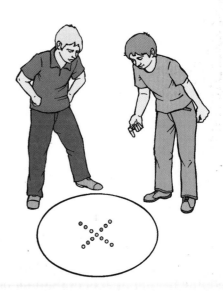

# CHARADES

Charades is perhaps the best-known of all party games. This game is not only great for exercising your brain, but it is also a fantastic way to build your self-confidence, and as you are moving around so much when performing, it can also help to keep you fit. The object of charades is to help your team guess the identity of a film, book, TV show, or famous person by giving them clues using only hand gestures. No words are allowed. The first steps are to make sure that everyone is familiar with the system of recognized clues and signs that are used to help guess the answer.

| SKILL LEVEL | ❄ |
|---|---|
| TIME REQUIRED | 1 hour |

**1** Go through the clues to indicate a book, film, and so on. For a book, hold your hands out flat with palms up and the edges of the palms touching one another, imitating an open book. If it is a TV program, draw a rectangle in the air, or for a film, make a ring shape with the thumb and forefinger of one hand, while making a cranking motion with the other hand, imitating a film camera. To indicate a famous person, strike a grand pose with one hand on your chest and the other arm outstretched theatrically.

**2** To mime to your teammates how many words are in the answer, hold up a number of fingers to indicate how many words you are trying to communicate; for example, if

miming the book *War and Peace*, you would hold up three. Follow it immediately by a second display of fingers to indicate which word you will tackle first: one for the "first word" two for "second word," and so on.

**3** Hold a number of fingers against your arm to indicate how many syllables a word has. Follow it immediately by a second display of fingers to indicate which syllable you will tackle first.

**4** Tug your earlobe to indicate that the word being guessed "sounds like" the word that you intend to mime. For example, if you are trying to get your team to guess the film "Jaws," you could tug your ear then make a "claws" shape with two hands.

## YOU WILL NEED

**Two teams of two players or more**

**A spacious area to play in, with comfy seating for the teams**

### DID YOU KNOW?

Charades dates back to 16th-century France, where popular parlor games called *Petit Jeux* (meaning "Little Games") were composed of intellectual exercises created for evening fun. It was so popular that even kings and queens played it. In 1654, King Louis XIV ballet danced the clues to a comedy of proverbs.

**5** Make a big circle in the air if you wish to indicate that you will try to mime the whole thing at once.

**6** To indicate that a member of your team has guessed correctly, point at that person while touching your nose with your other hand.

**7** Once you have gone through the clues and signals, split everyone into two teams. Each team must pick a member to be the first to mime its charade. Toss a coin to see which team goes first.

**8** When the order of play has been decided, the first "actor" steps up in front of the group. This person has three minutes to mime their charade. If the team hasn't guessed correctly within that time, it does not score a point. If the team guesses correctly, it scores one point. After the turn is concluded one way or the other, the other team takes its turn.

**9** The game continues for as long as everyone wants to play, but it can help to set a limit on the number of rounds at the start. Try starting with the same number of rounds as there are people in each team. Team members must all take turns to mime, one after the other.

# PICTIONARY

If you love charades, you can play a drawing version of it. You don't need to be an artist—you just need a pen, paper, and some friends.

| | |
|---|---|
| **SKILL LEVEL** | ❄ |
| **TIME NEEDED** | 1 hour |

## YOU WILL NEED

**Two teams of two players or more**

**A pencil, pen, and/or slim black marker**

**Paper**

**1** One team tells one member of the opposing team an image that he/she will have to draw without telling the other member(s) of the drawer's team.

**2** The drawer has to draw the image without using letters, numbers, or symbols. His/her team member(s) have to guess what the image is within a minute.

**3** A team scores a point if its team member(s) guesses the picture before the time is up. Each team takes turns drawing an image for their team member(s). The first team to score 10 points wins.

# HIDING GAMES

Some of the best indoor games involve concealing yourself in fiendishly hard-to-find places while someone tries to track you down. The best known of them all, hide-and-seek, can be played by as few as two people. Sardines is a variation on the same idea that is fun to play with a few friends.

| SKILL LEVEL | ❄ |
|---|---|
| TIME NEEDED | ½–1 hour |

## YOU WILL NEED

Two or more players

A safe environment to play in, like your home

## HIDE-AND-SEEK

**1** Draw straws to decide who will be the "hunter."

**2** While the hunter counts slowly to thirty with their eyes shut, the other players must run away to hide. Spaces under beds and behind curtains are all good places to try—use your imagination to find a spot that the hunter will never think of.

**3** After the hunter has reached a count of thirty, they may open their eyes and start looking for the other players. The last one to be found is the winner and becomes the hunter in the next round.

## SARDINES

Sardines is similar to hide-and-seek but works the opposite way. In this game, only one person goes off to hide at the start of the game. They must find a hiding place that is well tucked away, but big enough to hold more than one person.

**1** After a count of thirty, all the "hunting" players go off separately to look for the person in hiding.

**2** When one of the hunters finds the hider, they must not announce their discovery, but quietly join them in their hiding place instead.

**3** If another hunter discovers the hiding place, they must join the first two players there—and so on, until only one hunter is left. When they find the group of players in hiding, they win the game and become the first to hide in the next round.

# COIN TRICKS

If you like to mystify your friends and family, this is one of the simplest tricks in the magician's box, yet it looks very impressive when done correctly. The key to success is sleight of hand, so the advice is: practice, practice, practice.

SKILL LEVEL ✳ ✳ ✳

TIME REQUIRED 5 minutes

## DISAPPEARING COIN

**1** Place the coin on the table in full view of your audience and then turn the glass upside-down over the coin. Place the towel over the glass and, with as much drama as you can muster, move the glass around the table in circles.

**2** While sliding the glass around, very carefully maneuver it so that the coin slides off the table and into your lap (if you're sitting), or into your waiting hand. Remove the towel, and the coin has disappeared into thin air!

**YOU WILL NEED**

A drinking glass

A coin

A small hand towel

A table

A matchbox

## REAPPEARING COIN

**1** Before the show, open a matchbox halfway. Wedge a coin between the end of the drawer and the cover. As the applause from your disappearing coin trick dies down, produce the matchbox and, holding it tightly so the coin doesn't slip back into the box, show the audience that the box is "empty."

**2** Now close the matchbox, and the coin will slip down into it. Say a few magic words over the box, open it back up, and—abracadabra—your coin has magically reappeared!

# MAKING A BOUNCING EGG

It's easy to take everyday objects for granted, like an egg, for example. When you drop it on the floor it smashes, right? It doesn't in this intriguing science experiment—you can turn an ordinary hen's egg into something that behaves more like a rubber ball. The process behind this is a scientific phenomenon called osmosis, in which a highly concentrated liquid, in this case vinegar, passes through a porous wall (eggshell) and into the less concentrated material within (the egg white and yolk). As the process takes place you'll see bubbles forming on the surface of the egg—this is a sign that the calcium-based material of the shell is being broken down by the acid in the vinegar. You may also see parts of the dissolved eggshell floating on the surface.

**SKILL LEVEL**                 ❄

**TIME NEEDED**           1 week

**1** Boil an egg in a pan of water for 10 minutes, then remove and allow to cool.

**2** Place the egg inside a large glass jar and fill to the brim with white vinegar.

**3** Replace the lid on the jar and store it in a place where it will not be disturbed.

**4** Check the egg daily to watch the transformations happen.

**5** When a week has gone by, remove the lid of the jar, drain the vinegar away, and extract the egg.

You'll find that the shell has disappeared entirely, leaving a very rubbery egg.

**6** Try dropping the egg onto a hard surface from about knee height. It should actually bounce!

## YOU WILL NEED

A large jar with a screw-top lid

White vinegar

An egg

A saucepan

# INFINITY MIRRORS

The winter months can be a bit gloomy outside, but there's still plenty of fun to be had with indoor lights—including the mind-bogglingly marvelous infinity mirror. Mirrors can be found in nearly every home, but with a few tweaks, this familiar household object can be turned into a gateway to infinity!

| | |
|---|---|
| SKILL LEVEL | ❄ ❄ |
| TIME NEEDED | 1 hour |

**1** Use scissors to trim the mirrored foil to the same size as your sheet of Perspex.

**2** Apply the trimmed window foil to the Perspex, smoothing it out carefully to remove any bubbles. The Perspex should now be see-through on one side, but mirrored on the other.

**3** Using lengths of balsa wood of about an inch in depth, assemble a taped-together rectangular frame round the edges of the mirror, which should be shiny-side up. Carefully attach the fairy lights to the top edge of the frame with duct tape, fixing them at 1-inch (2.5-cm) intervals around its edge with the bulbs facing inwards. You should end up with something that looks like a mirror in a deep picture frame.

**4** Switch on the fairy lights, dim any other lighting in the room, and prepare for the exciting part. Take the sheet of Perspex and hold it mirrored-side down directly above the frame. Looking into its clear side, you should see an infinite tunnel of colored lights before you!

## YOU WILL NEED

A rectangular plastic or glass mirror

A sheet of Perspex (transparent plastic) cut to the same size as the mirror

Duct tape

A pair of scissors

Strips of balsa wood

A hacksaw (to cut balsa to length)

A serrated knife to cut polystyrene

Mirrored window foil

Battery-powered fairy lights

## WARNING

Make sure you get an adult to help you when using the saw and the knife. Sharp blades can be dangerous, and you shouldn't use these unsupervised.

## DID YOU KNOW?

Light is the fastest-moving thing in our universe, traveling at 186,282 miles (300,000 km) every second.

# BREAKING DOWN COLOR

Sometimes it seems as though scientific exploration is as much about learning big new words as it is learning about the world. "Chromatography" is one of those words. It refers to the study of colored dyes. You might wonder why scientists need to study color. Well, it is because almost all colored dyes are made by mixing other colors together. Take a packet of sugar-coated candies, for example. Each color in that packet is a combination of dyes—all you have to do is look on the ingredients list to see how many. We can use chromatography to discover what dyes make up each color in a packet of candies, by dissolving the dyes and separating them out with a few simple household items. The experiment requires some patience and attention to detail, but it can be done in about an hour.

**SKILL LEVEL**  ❋ ❋ ❋

**TIME REQUIRED**  1–2 hours

## YOU WILL NEED

A packet of sugar-coated candies in different colors

A paper coffee filter

A pair of scissors

A sheet of tin foil

Water

An eye dropper

Six tall glasses

Salt

A ruler

Tape

Six pencils

Six toothpicks

A large empty soda bottle with a cap

**1** Cut a rectangle out of your paper coffee filter. Using a ruler, measure ¼ inch (6 mm) up from the bottom of the rectangle and draw a pencil line all the way across. Then cut the rectangle lengthways into 1-inch- (2.5-cm-) wide strips.

**2** You should cut out as many strips of paper as you have different colors of candy, and each piece should have the pencil line drawn across the bottom.

**3** Just underneath each line, use your pencil to make a dot. Then, label one dot for each different color of candy

you have (for example, you might mark Y for yellow, G for green, BL for blue, BR for brown, R for red, and O for orange).

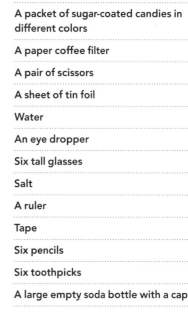

**4** Set the coffee filter strips aside and get out a sheet of tin foil. Using an eye-dropper, put six drops of water on the foil. Space them far enough apart so that they don't run into each other.

**5** Next, put a different colored candy on each drop of water. After about a minute or two, the water will dissolve the colored dye off the candy. Once all the dye has come off the candies, carefully remove them so that you're left with colored drops of water.

**6** Next, dip the tip of a toothpick into the colored drop and lightly touch it to the corresponding labeled dot on a coffee filter strip. You don't need much dye at all, so keep the dot of color small. Be sure to use a different toothpick for each color.

**7** Wait for the spots to dry and repeat step 6 two more times for each color, letting the spots dry each time before adding more dye.

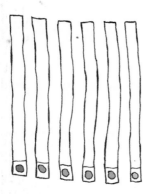

## CHROMATOGRAPHY

Chromatography works because all the different colors in the dyes are made up of different-sized particles, some of which dissolve better than others in water. The water dissolves all the dyes together when it reaches the colored spot, but as the level of water creeps up, the water starts to evaporate off the paper. Because there is less water to carry them along, the dyes that are hardest to dissolve drop out of solution and stay on the paper, giving you a colored mark, while the rest of the colors move on. Each dye drops out at a different point, showing you clearly exactly what dyes have gone into the overall color.

If you are having trouble getting the colors to separate, you may need to give them more space. Try a longer piece of paper and a taller glass, and leave the process to work overnight. If you still can't see any colors separating out, then the dye probably only has one color in it.

**8** When the spots have dried completely, fold the top end of each strip over the middle of a pencil and tape it in place.

**9** Then, balance each pencil on top of a glass, so that the strip hangs down with the colored dots near the bottom of the glass.

**10** Create a salt "developing" solution by mixing 3 cups (750 ml) of water and 1 teaspoon of salt in a large soda bottle. Shake the bottle well until all the salt has dissolved.

**11** Pour the salt solution into each glass until it just covers the bottom of each strip. Don't let the level of solution reach the colored dot, or it'll just wash off the dye.

**12** Here's the fun part: Watch as the filter absorbs the water, and the dots of dye begin to separate into the many colors used to make that dye up.

**13** Once the filters have absorbed enough water and the colors all seem to have separated, pull the strips out of the glasses and lay them on a table side by side to dry. Now you can see that the colors of each candy are actually made up of lots of different dyes.

**DID YOU KNOW?**

The darker a dye is, the more different colors have probably gone into it. Dark blue and black dyes are usually made up of the most colors. This is because dyes work by absorbing wavelengths of light that our eyes see as color. Dark colors absorb more wavelengths than light colors, and mixing lots of different dyes together is an easy way to make sure more wavelengths are absorbed.

# STATIC ELECTRICITY

Shuffle your feet across a nylon-carpeted floor, and you get a shock when you touch a door knob. Rub a balloon on your head and your hair stands on end, while the balloon will stick to the wall. What's the connection? It's called static electricity. Static electricity is created when an object loses its electrical balance.

Everything in the universe is made up of tiny particles called atoms, which are themselves made up of even tinier particles called protons, electrons, and neutrons. Protons have a positive electrical charge, electrons have a negative one, and neutrons have no charge at all. Even our own bodies are made up of these charged particles—the reason we don't go around sparking like frayed electrical wires is because the negative and positive charges in us offset each other, giving us (and most other objects) a neutral charge overall.

Static electricity is created when the balance gets out of whack. When two objects are rubbed together the electrons in one can sometimes jump to the other, causing the object that lost the electrons to become positively charged, and the object that gained the electrons to become negatively charged. This separation of charged particles is called static electricity.

So why do you get a shock if you touch a door knob after walking across the carpet? Because some of the electrons in the rug have jumped to you, giving you a small negative charge. When you touch the door knob, the shock you feel is the energy released by extra electrons in your body moving to the neutral door knob.

Your hair stands on end when you rub a balloon on it for a slightly different reason. Opposite electrical charges attract, and similar electrical charges push away from each other, just like the poles on a magnet. The friction of rubbing causes some of the electrons in your hair to jump to the balloon, giving each hair on your head a positive charge. That causes each hair to try and get away from the others, and the furthest away they can get is to stand up straight.

**DID YOU KNOW?**

Photocopiers use static electricity to attach toner powder to the page in the form of the image that's being copied. They then fix the powder to the page by heating it.

# BENDING WATER

You can see the same process in other experiments. In this one, for example, you can use static electricity to bend a stream of water.

| | |
|---|---|
| **SKILL LEVEL** | ❄ ❄ |
| **TIME NEEDED** | 20 minutes |

**1** Turn on the water faucet to get a small stream of water. The thinner the stream, the easier it'll be to make it bend.

**2** Run the comb through your hair about five times. Some of the electrons from your hair will transfer to the comb, giving it a negative charge (your hair will likely stand up with repelling positive charges).

**3** Carefully bring the comb close to the stream of water, but don't let them touch. The negative charge of the comb will attract the positive charge of the water molecules, thereby bending the stream of water toward the comb.

**4** If the water touches the comb, the static charge will dissipate and the effect will be lost. If you can't get a charge off your hair, try stroking the comb with a fleece jacket to build up static.

## YOU WILL NEED

A plastic hair comb

A water faucet

## DID YOU KNOW?

Thunder and lightning are caused by static electricity. If you build up a big static charge, you can hear a crackling noise and see a small flash when it discharges. (Try taking off a woolen sweater or fleece in a dark room and you'll be able to see the flashes.) Thunder and lightning are exactly the same, only much, much bigger. The static charge is thought to be caused by water and ice particles in thunder clouds colliding and transferring electrons.

# JUGGLING

Juggling is lots of fun and a great way to impress your friends, and it can keep you entertained for hours. Master this simple method, and the next thing you know you'll be auditioning for the circus. Juggling is difficult at the start, so build up in stages. Here are some exercises to get you going.

**SKILL LEVEL** ❄ ❄ ❄

**TIME NEEDED** 1–2 hours

## YOU WILL NEED

Three round, light objects of equal size, or professionally made juggling balls

## BEGINNER

**1** Hold two balls in your right hand and one in your left. Throw one ball from your right hand and catch it in the left.

**2** Throw the ball back from your left hand and catch it in your right. Easy so far, right?

**3** Practice until you never drop any of the balls. When you're feeling confident, move onto the next stage.

## INTERMEDIATE

**1** Again, start with two balls held in your right hand and one ball held in your left.

**2** Throw one ball from your right hand as you did for the beginner's practice. As it reaches the top of its arc, throw the ball in your left hand.

**3** Catch the first ball you threw in your left hand, and the second ball you threw in your right hand. The two balls should have exchanged places.

**4** Again, practice this until you can do it without ever dropping a ball.

## ADVANCED

**1** Put two balls in your right hand and one in your left. Start by throwing one of the balls in your right hand up and slightly to the left.

**2** Then throw the ball in your left hand up and under the ball you just threw, as you did in the intermediate step.

**3** As you catch the first ball in your left hand throw the last ball in the air and catch the second ball with your right hand.

**4** You are essentially playing catch with all three balls at the same time, so there's always a third ball in the air.

**5** This can be pretty difficult to start with, so keep practicing—count the number of throws you can manage before dropping any of the balls to see how well you're doing.

# INDOOR OBSTACLE COURSE

An indoor obstacle course will provide enough thrills and spills to keep you entertained and amused when it's cold and windy outside. An obstacle course puts all of your physical skills to the test: you'll need agility, speed, and good coordination, plus plenty of energy and determination. With a little careful planning, you can design your own indoor course that is fun and fiendishly challenging. First, ask an adult for permission to use a room or two in your house to construct the course in. Things may have to be moved around a bit to create the various obstacles. Ask your family what furniture is okay to use. Chairs and tables are good for making into obstacles, as are couches and throws. Avoid fragile things and appliances like TV sets, as these are easily broken.

## THE OBSTACLES

By including some of the obstacles suggested below, and maybe adding one or two of your own, you can build a course that has a wide variety of tricky tasks to complete. When you've given it a couple of trial runs, try timing competitors from start to finish. That way, you can create a "leader board" of fastest overall times. Below are a few tricky obstacles to try. You can link them together however you want, but it's usually good to start with a chair zig-zag and end with the tongue twister.

**CHAIR ZIG-ZAG** Place four chairs in a straight line with narrow gaps between them. Competitors must zig-zag between them before moving on to the next obstacle.

**HULA SPIN** Competitors must pick up a hula hoop from the floor and spin it around their middle five times before moving on to the next obstacle.

| SKILL LEVEL | ❄ ❄ |
|---|---|
| TIME NEEDED | 1–2 hours |

### YOU WILL NEED

A room or rooms to build the course in

Dining chairs

A skipping rope

Balloons

Quilt

A lightweight pole (for the limbo dance)

A hula-hoop

Wastepaper baskets

Plastic cups

Candies

**LIMBO DANCE** Balance a lightweight pole between two chair backs of equal height. Competitors must "limbo" under it—walk while bending over backwards low enough to pass beneath the bar (without using hands or knees to aid balance). If the bar is knocked off, the competitor must start again. They can have up to a total of three attempts.

**PAPER BALL TOSS** Place three wastepaper baskets (or similar) at varying distances from a line on the floor. Without crossing the line, competitors must throw a ball of scrunched up wastepaper into each of the baskets before moving on.

**QUILT TUNNEL** Place a duvet on the floor and weight it down along its longer edges with books or similar. Contestants must wriggle underneath the duvet tunnel and emerge from the other side before continuing to the next obstacle.

**SKIPPING ROPE HOP** Jump rope five times before moving on.

**TREASURE HUNT** Stand ten plastic cups on the floor upside down. Hide a candy (this is the "treasure") under one of them when the contestant isn't looking. The contestant must discover which one the "treasure"' is hidden under by lifting them up one by one. The contestant MUST return empty cups to an upright position after checking them. This challenges memory skills and means you can't cheat by knocking all the cups over at once to find the candy.

**BALLOON POP** This is a good one to save for near the end, as it makes lots of noise! Blow up five party balloons.

Contestants must pop them all by jumping on them before continuing.

**TONGUE TWISTER** It's nice to end the course with an exercise that will test your gift of gab: a tongue twister. Contestants must repeat the phrase: "I want to win the wonderful winter wrangle outright" five times without making any mistakes before they can cross the finish line.

# MAKING A TELEPHONE

Most people think telephones are complex machines, but the landline phone in your house is one of the simplest devices around. In fact, the technology hasn't changed too much since it was invented in the 1870s (although mobile phone and wireless technology is a different story). Essentially, when a person speaks into a phone, their voice vibrates a membrane. Those sound vibrations are transferred along the phone line to another phone, where they are recreated identically through another membrane that acts as a speaker. In a phone line, the vibrations are carried electrically, but you can recreate this physically using string telephones.

| | |
|---|---|
| SKILL LEVEL | ❄ ❄ |
| TIME NEEDED | 15 minutes |

**1** Use the needle to poke a hole through the center at the bottom of each of your two cups.

**2** Push one end of the string up through each hole, and tie it to a paper clip so the string doesn't slip out of the cup.

**3** Give one cup to a friend and get far enough apart so that the string is stretched out taut between you.

**4** Talk and listen into the cups. Vibrations from your voice should be carried along the string to the cup at the other end.

## YOU WILL NEED

A sewing needle

Two paper cups

A long piece of string

Two paper clips

## DID YOU KNOW?

Alexander Graham Bell is known as the father of the telephone. In reality, however, the invention of the telephone system is credited to a number of people. It was Bell who managed to successfully patent the telephone as an "apparatus for transmitting vocal or other sounds telegraphically." However in 1860, sixteen years prior to the filing of the patent, Antonio Meucci had demonstrated a device that he called the "teletrofono" in New York.

# ROPE GAMES

You don't need expensive gadgets and gizmos to have a lot of fun. These rope games, for example, require only a length of cord and some energetic players. Rope is, by its nature, very versatile stuff. Just like a deck of cards, you can take a simple length of rope—preferably a lightweight, pliable variety that's easy to handle—and adapt it to use in a number of games. Try some of the suggestions below next time you're stuck inside and want something fun to do.

| | |
|---|---|
| SKILL LEVEL | ❋ ❋ |
| TIME NEEDED | ½ hour each |

**WEB RACER** Arrange ropes on the ground so they form a number of large, overlapping circles. One player is selected as the "spider" and the others are the "flies." The spider must try to catch the flies, but the job is made more difficult by the fact that the players must only walk on the ropes. If anyone steps off the ropes, pushes past another player, or is caught by the spider, they are out. The last fly to avoid being captured becomes the spider next time around.

**KNOT GAME** This activity is ideal for parties, or for any occasion when there is a large number (15–20) of people. Take a long rope—over 33 feet (10 m) in length—and tie a loose overhand (granny) knot in it for every person who is taking part. Make sure that the knots are evenly spaced out, about 24 inches (60 cm) apart. Each player must then choose a knot to stand beside, grasping a part of the rope next to their knot with one hand. The aim of the game is to untie every knot in the rope without letting go of the rope with the hand players are holding it with —and using only their free hand to untie the knots. Hint: Teamwork is essential to complete this game successfully.

**YOU WILL NEED**

Lightweight ropes of varying lengths

A skipping rope

Six or more people

# STORY GAMES

When it's dark outside but the fire is burning indoors and all is cozy, it's a great time to play story games. With actions to perform as well as tales to hear, this activity is energetic and exciting. The tradition of winter storytelling goes back thousands of years. People of the world's earliest cultures would gather together in the warmth of their houses to spend the hours of a long night by telling stories. Today, story games still have the power to fascinate and amuse—here are two modern ones that are great fun to play the next time you have a few friends around.

| SKILL LEVEL | ❄ |
| TIME NEEDED | ½ hour each |

## YOU WILL NEED

Pre-prepared stories

Six or more participants

Candies for the winners

## RUMORS

**1** For this classic game, everyone must sit in a circle. The storyteller whispers a very short tale to the person next to them. It should contain unusual events, objects and details, but should not take more than a minute or so to tell. For example, you could tell a quick story about how six monkeys stole six things from you as you went for a walk in a park.

**2** The player next to you must try to remember as many details as

possible and then whisper the story to the person next to them, recalling as many details as possible.

**3** When the last person in the circle has heard the story, they must tell it out loud to the group. You'll be surprised how much it has changed from the original!

## TRUE OR FALSE

Each player must tell a story about themselves, and the other players must decide if it is true or false by a majority decision. The story should be amusing and unusual but—in the case that a player is making it up—not so fantastic that no one could possibly believe it. If the storyteller succeeds in fooling the listeners into thinking it is real when it is false, or vice versa, they win a candy.

# PICKING UP AN ICE CUBE WITH A MATCH

When you announce to your friends that you plan to pick up an ice cube with a match, they'll probably think you've figured out a way to balance the cube on top of the match. Actually, it's much easier than that.

| | |
|---|---|
| **SKILL LEVEL** | ❄ |
| **TIME REQUIRED** | 15 minutes |

**1** Fill the bowl with water and float an ice cube in it.

**2** Lay the match on top of the cube. Be sure to leave a small portion of the match hanging off the side so you'll be able to grab it later.

**3** Pour salt on top of the ice cube around the match.

**4** Wait 3 minutes, then grab the match and pick it up, along with the ice cube stuck to it.

## YOU WILL NEED

A small bowl

Water

An ice cube

Salt

A match

## THE SCIENCE

The secret? Water normally freezes at 32°F (0°C). But when you dissolve salt in water, it won't freeze until it reaches 20°F (-7°C). When you sprinkle salt onto the top of the ice cube, it dissolves a little and melts the top of the cube by lowering the temperature at which water turns to ice. However, once the ice on top of the cube has melted, the salt washes off into the bowl of water and the top of the ice cube quickly refreezes, trapping the matchstick so it sticks to the ice.

### DID YOU KNOW?

One of the dangers of seas near the North and South Poles is that the salt in the water means they can stay liquid at very low temperatures. Anybody falling into the water loses their body heat very quickly, which can be fatal.

# TESTING MAGNETS

Playing with magnets is fun—at least it is for a while. But after the first few times, tricks like picking up a box-load of paper clips or sticking a picture to the refrigerator kind of lose their attraction. But what if you could use a magnet to power a boat? Since the opposite poles of two magnets always pull toward each other, you can use the forces between them as a source of power for a small model craft. It may sound silly, but magnet power will have your ship sailing in no time. Since the opposite poles of two magnets always pull toward each other, you can use the forces between them as a source of power for a small model craft.

| | |
|---|---|
| **SKILL LEVEL** | ❄ ❄ |
| **TIME NEEDED** | 40 minutes |

**1** Screw the eyelet screw into the middle of the bottom of the boat.

**2** Unfold a paper clip and hook one end through the eyelet on the bottom of the boat.

**3** The rest of the paper clip should hang straight down from the boat—make sure it isn't too long or the boat won't fit in a shallow baking dish.

**4** Use waterproof glue to stick one magnet securely to the bottom of the paper clip.

**5** Once the glue has dried, fill a baking dish with water and then float the boat in the dish. Make sure you fill it with enough water so

## YOU WILL NEED

A small wooden boat

An eyelet screw

A paper clip

Two small magnets

Waterproof glue

A rectangular glass baking dish

Water

## DID YOU KNOW?

The world's strongest permanent magnets (which are often called "supermagnets") are made from the alloy neodymium. A supermagnet that is just the size of a quarter can be used to lift a weight of more than 20 pounds (10 kg)!

## WARNING

Don't leave your magnet in the water overnight, in case it starts to rust.

that the magnet stays just above the bottom of the dish.

**6** Run a magnet slowly along the outside bottom of the baking dish. It will attract the magnet suspended from the boat and pull the boat in any direction you want.

## MAGNETIC FIELDS

The top speed of your magnetic boat probably isn't that high. So you might be surprised to hear that scientists are working to develop a magnetic drive to power real ships through the water.

The drive works on a principle called "magnetohydrodynamics," and it uses electricity running through saltwater in the presence of a magnetic field to create movement. Unfortunately, it's pretty slow at the moment—the only completed prototype was built in Japan in 1991 and could barely manage 9 miles per hour (15 kmph). In theory, however, a system like this could be used in the future to power ships reliably and efficiently. These engines would also be silent, making them ideal for powering submarines, which need to move very quietly so they don't give away their position.

# FREEZING WATER

Fresh water turns to ice when at temperatures of 32°F (0°C) or less. But if you add salt to water, it develops amazing powers of resistance to freezing.

| | |
|---|---|
| **SKILL LEVEL** | ❄ |
| **TIME NEEDED** | 24 hours |

### YOU WILL NEED

Two 2-pint (1-liter) containers

Water

Pen and paper to label the dishes

Salt

**1** Next time it is forecast to freeze overnight, fill two 2-pint (1-liter) containers with fresh water. Label one "No Salt" and the other "Salty."

**2** Add 5 heaped tablespoons of salt to one labeled "Salty." Make sure it is well stirred in.

**3** Set both containers outside at sundown. When you return to them in the morning, the "No Salt" dish should have frozen over, while the salty dish remains liquid—unless you've experienced exceptionally cold weather, in which case both will freeze eventually. If no cold weather is forecast, put the dishes in the freezer instead.

# SPINNING TOPS

Another easy project to make is a spinning top. What's fun about this is the decoration and shape of the top, and what it looks like while it's spinning. Or, if you're in a more competitive mood you can make fighting tops and have competitions with your friends. You can make your tops square, round, or triangular. Try painting them in different colors or patterns. Spirals on round tops can play tricks on the eyes once they get going.

| SKILL LEVEL | ❄ ❄ |
|---|---|
| TIME NEEDED | 40 minutes each |

## MAKING A DECORATIVE TOP

**1** Cut the shape of your top or tops out of the cardboard. You can make them any shape you like, but remember, if it's too heavy on one side it might not spin evenly.

**2** Decorate the top with bright colors and patterns. Try different patterns and see what effect is produced when you spin them.

**3** Push a wooden skewer through the center of the top. Leave most of the skewer above the cardboard, and just a short amount below it where the sharp tip of the skewer touches the ground. Glue or tape the skewer to secure it in place.

**4** To spin the top, use your fingers and give it a quick twist by rolling the skewer between your thumb and middle finger as if you were snapping.

### YOU WILL NEED

**Thick cardboard**

**Wooden skewers**

**A pair of scissors**

**Glue or tape**

# MAKING A FIGHTING TOP

You might find cardboard tops a bit lightweight for fighting, so experiment with tops made out of cork, wooden dowel, or plastic. Try different designs with different materials and see if you can build a winner. Here's one way to do it.

**1** Drill a hole ¼ in (5 mm) across, right down the center of your thick piece of dowel, so you're left with a wooden ring. This will be the body of your top.

**2** Use your knife to trim the short end of the thin dowel to a point, so your top can spin on it. (Or, you can use an ordinary pencil sharpener to make the point, if you want a shortcut.)

**3** Put a dab of glue on the end of a matchstick and smear it inside the hole in the thick dowel.

**4** Push the length of narrow dowel into the hole so it sticks out about ¼ in (5 mm) on the other side. Quickly wipe off any glue on the protruding end before it dries.

**5** When the glue dries, paint your top or use your knife to carve designs on it and streamline its shape however you want. Make a couple of tops yourself, or encourage your friends to make their own so you can challenge them.

## YOU WILL NEED

A 1-in (2-cm) length of a 1-in (2-cm) thick dowel

A drill with a ¼-in (5-mm) bit

A 2-in (4-cm) length of a ¼-in (5-mm) thick dowel

Wood glue

A knife

### WARNING

Only use the drill and the knife with adult supervision, or let an adult do those steps for you.

# TOP FIGHTS

**1** With your chalk or a stick, mark out a circle about 1 ft (30 cm) in diameter on a piece of flat ground.

**2** You and a friend each take a top and set them spinning as fast as you can in the ring. Then steer them into each other by blowing on them. When they collide, they'll go spinning off in different directions.

**3** The winner is the top that knocks the other one over or pushes it out of the ring, but keeps on spinning itself.

## YOU WILL NEED

Two tops

A friend to compete with

Chalk, or something else to mark out a ring

Flat ground

# MEMORY GAME

When the weather's too cold and wet to play outside, try giving your brain some exercise with this classic brain teaser. The ability to remember things quickly and accurately is a very handy skill. Just as your body becomes stronger the more exercise you do, your memory skills will improve the more you use them.

| | |
|---|---|
| SKILL LEVEL | ❄ ❄ |
| TIME NEEDED | 15 minutes |

**1** Assemble twenty common household objects: small things like buttons, coins, and erasers are good. You can also throw in a couple of oddities that might be harder to memorize, like an unusual paperweight or piece of jewelry.

**2** Place the objects on a table and cover them with a cloth.

**3** Gather together a group of players and give them all a notepad and pen to write with.

**4** Remove the cloth from the objects for one minute. Players may not make notes during this time, but they must try to memorize as many of the objects as possible. After the minute has elapsed, the objects must be covered again.

**5** The player who correctly recalls the greatest number of objects, jotting them down on the pad afterwards, wins the game.

## YOU WILL NEED

An assortment of around twenty small objects

A cloth

A surface to play on

Pens and paper

## DID YOU KNOW?

The Ancient Greeks invented a memory technique that is still a very effective way to recall facts in the right order. In your imagination, think of a route you travel everyday (say, a walk to school), and place objects or facts to be memorized beside familiar landmarks along the way. If you're trying to remember the names of famous U.S. Presidents in the order they took office, for example, you might imagine George Washington standing at the end of your drive and Thomas Jefferson a little further on beside a familiar shop—and so on, all along the route. Try it; it really works.

## TOP TIP

For a tasty variation on the game, use sweets, fruit, and other healthy snack items as your objects. The winner gets the first pick from the items afterwards, and the rest are then shared around the group.

# MIME HANDS

At the theater, actors work together to bring fictional stories to life. The art of mime goes one step further, because the actors use only gestures to tell a story. This fun game combines storytelling, miming, and teamwork. The aim is for one person to tell a story while their partner mimes the actions, but there's a twist—the person miming the actions has to act as the "hands" of the person telling the story.

| | |
|---|---|
| **SKILL LEVEL** | ❄ ❄ |
| **TIME NEEDED** | 10 minutes |

**1** Form players into teams of two. When it's your team's turn, the person telling the story must stand in front of the audience with their hands clasped behind their back.

**2** Their partner must step up behind them and thread their own hands through the arms of the storyteller so they poke out in front and look like the storyteller's real hands.

**3** The storyteller must then tell a story. Simple tales about everyday activities—such as getting ready to go to school or making dinner—work best.

**4** Meanwhile, their partner, who is acting as the storyteller's hands, mimes the actions that are taking place in the story, such as using a knife and fork, doing up a necktie, and so on. Done properly, the effect is eerily lifelike—and very funny.

## YOU WILL NEED

**Teams of two players**

**An active imagination!**

## DID YOU KNOW?

Charlie Chaplin is perhaps the most famous mime actor that ever lived. In the early days of the 20th century, films didn't have any sound, but Chaplin—with his trademark bowler hat and cane—made classic comic films using actions alone, and he was loved by audiences worldwide. His 1925 film *The Gold Rush* made $4.25 million at the box office.

# CUP AND BALL TRICKS

Here's a good, clean magic trick that's been making the magician's circuit for centuries. Like most good tricks, it can be done quite simply, but it has a big impact. What you'll do is seemingly pass paper balls magically through the end of a cup after stacking them all up together. You don't need any special skills or materials to perform this trick, and anyone who has about 30 minutes to practice should be able to pull it off.

| | |
|---|---|
| **SKILL LEVEL** | ❄❄ |
| **TIME NEEDED** | ½ hour |

**1** Tear the napkin into four equal-sized pieces and screw them up into four small paper balls.

**2** Secretly put one of those paper balls inside a plastic cup and turn the cup over on the table with the ball underneath. Don't let anyone see you do this.

**3** Turn the two remaining cups upside down on either side of that cup and lay out the remaining three balls in plain sight in front of the cups.

**4** Start the trick by placing one of those three balls on top of the middle cup (the one with the secret ball under it). Tell your audience that you are going to make the ball pass by magic through the bottom of the cup and land on the table top.

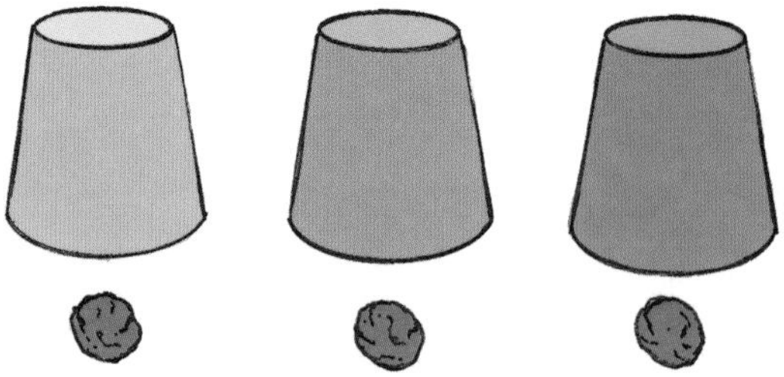

### YOU WILL NEED

- A paper napkin
- Three opaque (not transparent) plastic cups

**5** Then stack the other two cups over the ball. When all three cups are stacked, say a few magic words and tap the top of the stack.

**10** Now you can do the whole thing again: place one of the remaining balls on top of the middle cup (the one with the two secret balls under it), then place another ball on top of the middle cup and put the third cup on top.

**6** Lift the stack up to reveal the ball underneath—it looks as though the ball you put inside has magically passed through the cup.

**7** Continue by removing the cups and placing them upside down on the table.

**8** As you remove the second cup, remember that there is a ball under it that your audience doesn't know about. Let the ball slide into the second cup as you take it off the stack—you can pretend that the cups are stuck together to cover for this. Then turn this cup over quickly so that the ball doesn't fall out.

**9** Make this cup the middle cup and put it down on top of the first ball you "magically" made appear. Now there should be two balls under the cup although everyone will think there's only one.

**11** When all three cups are stacked, say a few magic words and tap the top of the stack.

**12** Lift the stack up to reveal two balls underneath— again, it looks as though the ball you put inside has magically passed through the cup. Lift up the second cup to show that the ball is still there.

**13** Repeat the process a third time, and all three balls will appear under the cup. Stack all the cups up together on top of the balls so the secret fourth ball stays hidden, and take a bow.

# FEASTING

When the weather outside calls for staying indoors, there is nothing more delightful and satisfying than being in a warm kitchen creating delicious dishes. Whether it's a filling main course like our hearty Irish stew, or a seasonal traditional treat such as candy apples, there's something in this chapter to please every cooking enthusiast. So don't worry what the weather is up to—here are some mouth-watering recipes for every meal and occassion to keep you happily preparing, cooking, baking, and decorating.

# CARROT CAKE

Packed full of fruit and vegetables—yes, vegetables!—this moist cake is simply irresistible. It's quick and easy to make and tastes delicious with or without the creamy topping. Carrots have been used in sweet cakes since the Middle Ages. Back then, sweeteners were hard to come by and expensive, while carrots—which contain more sugar than any other vegetable besides the sugar beet—were much easier to get and were used to make sweet desserts. But this cake has stood the test of time, and it is still a popular dessert today.

**1** Preheat the oven to 375°F (190°C) and lightly grease a baking tin.

**2** Place the pan on doubled greaseproof paper and draw around the base. Carefully cut out two layers of greaseproof paper to line the bottom of the pan.

**3** Grate or zest the peel of the orange and then squeeze out its juice using a lemon squeezer. Put the zest and juice to one side while you make the cake mix.

**4** In a large mixing bowl, mix the butter and sugar together until light and fluffy.

**5** Add the eggs one at a time and beat in to the mixture.

**6** Add the flour slowly and fold into the mixture using the metal spoon.

## SKILL LEVEL / TIME NEEDED

| SKILL LEVEL | ❄ ❄ |
|---|---|
| TIME NEEDED | 1 hour |

## YOU WILL NEED

**FOR THE CAKE:**

⅔ cup (140 g) butter or margarine

⅔ cup (140 g) soft brown sugar

2 large eggs

2 cups (225 g) self-rising flour

2 teaspoons baking powder (or ½ teaspoon baking soda and 1 teaspoon cream of tartar)

1 orange

1 ½ cups (175 g) grated carrot

½ teaspoon vanilla extract

⅓ cup (55 g) golden raisins

Orange zester or fine grater and lemon squeezer

Mixing bowl

Wooden spoon or handheld electric mixer

Metal spoon

7 in (18 cm) square baking pan

Greaseproof paper

## DID YOU KNOW?

Even though carrots have been used in cooking as a sweetener since medieval times, it was not until the 1960s that Viola Schlicting from Texas created the first recognized carrot cake, derived from a German carrot-nut bread recipe. Now carrot cake is a firm favorite in every coffee shop and bakery.

**7** In the same way, fold in the baking powder (or baking soda and cream of tartar), orange zest and juice, grated carrot, vanilla extract, and raisins. If the grated carrot is soggy, pat it dry with paper towel before adding it to the mixture.

**8** When all the ingredients are well combined, scoop the mixture into the prepared pan.

**9** Bake in the middle of the preheated oven for 45–50 minutes until the cake is golden brown.

**10** Using oven mitts, carefully remove the cake from the oven and allow to cool in the pan before taking it out.

**11** While the cake is cooling, you can make the icing, if you want to add this step.

**12** To make the icing, put all the ingredients into a mixing bowl and blend well together until the mixture is smooth.

**13** Once the cake is completely cooled, remove it from the baking pan, spread the topping thickly over the cake, and serve.

## YOU WILL NEED

FOR THE ICING:

1 cup (210 g) cream cheese

¼ cup (57 g) unsalted butter, softened

¼ cup (48 g) sifted icing sugar

1 teaspoon orange essence

Mixing bowl

Wooden spoon or handheld electric mixer

## TOP TIP

This cake will stay fresh for a few days in an airtight container—that's if you can resist it for that long!

# FRUIT CAKE

Lots of kids find fruit cake a bit heavy, but wait until your friends try this yummy version. It is so moist, light, and packed full of fruit that they won't be able to resist coming back for another slice. And unlike traditional fruit cakes, it really is quick and easy to make. When buying the dried fruit and candied peel for this recipe, look for the natural, unsulfered variety—it will make this cake much healthier.

**1** Preheat the oven to 350°F (180°C) and lightly grease the baking pan. Line the base and sides with two layers of greaseproof paper.

**2** Put the butter or margarine, sugar, fruit, water, fruit juice, baking soda, and mixed spice into a saucepan over moderate heat. Bring to a boil and then simmer for 1 minute.

**3** Pour into a mixing bowl and allow to cool.

**4** Once cooled, add eggs, flour and salt, and mix well.

**5** Pour mixture into a lined pan. Bake for around 1 ¼ hours (if top of cake starts to brown too much,

put some brown paper over the top to stop it from burning).

**6** To test if the cake is ready, insert a toothpick in the middle of the cake. If it comes out clean, the cake is ready.

**7** Remove from the pan, remove the greaseproof paper, and leave to cool on a wire rack.

**8** Unlike many rich fruit cakes, this delicious version is ready to eat right away. However, if you wanted to use this recipe for a Christmas cake, it is certainly special enough. Simply cover in marzipan and then ice it.

## TOP TIP

If you wrap the cake in tin foil and keep it in an airtight tin, it will stay fresh for a couple of months.

| SKILL LEVEL | ❄ ❄ |
| --- | --- |
| TIME NEEDED | 1 hour |

### YOU WILL NEED

2 ½ cups (340 g) mixed dried fruit (including raisins, candied peel, cherries—whatever you like)

½ cup (120 ml) white grape juice

½ cup (120 ml) water

½ cup (120 g) all-purpose flour

½ cup (120 g) cup self-rising flour

Pinch of salt

1 teaspoon baking soda

½ teaspoon mixed spice

½ cup (120 g) unsalted butter or margarine, softened

⅔ cup (170 g) sugar

2 large eggs, beaten

Large saucepan

Mixing bowl

Wooden spoon or handheld electric mixer

Metal spoon

7 in (18 cm) square or 8 in (20 cm) round cake pan

Greaseproof paper

# GINGERBREAD PEOPLE

You are never too old to enjoy making and eating gingerbread people. This recipe has just the right amount of ginger to make them flavorful but not too strong. It is great fun for a sleepover, and when they're done, you get to eat them while watching a movie with friends! This recipe will make about twelve gingerbread people.

| | |
|---|---|
| **SKILL LEVEL** | ❄ ❄ |
| **TIME NEEDED** | 45 minutes–1 hour |

**1** Sift the flour, baking soda, and ground ginger together in a mixing bowl.

**2** Chop the butter into small pieces, and rub into dry mixture to form what looks like fine breadcrumbs.

**3** Add the sugar and mix together.

**4** Mix the beaten egg and light corn syrup together, and gradually add to the dry mixture, mixing together to form a dough.

**5** On a floured surface, roll dough out to about ¼ inch (3 mm) thick. Using a cookie cutter, cut out as many "people" as you can.

**6** Remaining scraps can be balled together and rolled out again to cut out more "people."

**7** Place on a lightly greased baking sheet, and bake for approximately 10 to 15 minutes or until golden brown.

**8** When cooked, take out of the oven and leave on a baking sheet for a few minutes, then transfer to a cooling rack.

**9** Add decorations, and then leave to cool completely.

## YOU WILL NEED

3 ½ cups (340 g) all-purpose flour

1 teaspoon baking soda

2 ½ teaspoons ground ginger

½ cup (113 g) unsalted butter

¾ cups (170 g) light brown soft sugar

1 egg, beaten

4 tablespoons light corn syrup

Currants or small sweets (to decorate)

A mixing bowl

A sieve

A rolling pin

A gingerbread person cookie cutter

A greased baking sheet

# CANDY APPLES

Nights around the campfire just wouldn't be the same without candy apples. They are always a popular treat at festivals and carnivals and are perfect for any winter parties you're throwing at home. Or, since they are fun and so simple to make, you can brighten up any gloomy winter's day by making a batch of these lovely, bright treats.

| SKILL LEVEL | ❄ |
|---|---|
| TIME NEEDED | 3 hours |

**1** Push the wooden popsicle sticks halfway into the apples, near the stalk.

**2** Place sugar and water in the saucepan and dissolve over a medium heat.

**3** Add butter, syrup, and food coloring (if using), and slowly bring to a boil to create toffee.

**4** Allow to boil without stirring until the toffee cracks softly.

**5** Remove pan from the heat and carefully dip each apple into the toffee, turning them so that they are completely coated.

**6** Let them stand on a baking tray lined with parchment paper and allow to harden.

## YOU WILL NEED

6 popsicle sticks

6 apples (red and/or green)

1¼ cup (225 g) granulated sugar

½ cup (110 ml) water

A heavy-based saucepan

1½ tablespoons (30 g) butter

2 tablespoons light corn syrup

Red food coloring (optional)

A baking tray

Parchment paper

### DID YOU KNOW?

In France, toffee apples are called "pommes d'amour"—literally translated, this means "apples of love."

### WARNING

Be very careful when dipping the apples so that you don't get the hot toffee mixture on you, as it will stick to your skin and burn you.

# MIXED BERRY JELLY

You can't beat homemade jellies spread thick on toast or scones on cold winter mornings. Making jelly is the ideal way to preserve the taste and nutritional value of summer fruits so that they can be enjoyed throughout the year. It also ensures that a lot of fruit will not go to waste if you have more than you can eat, and jelly will last a good long while. In this simple and quick recipe, you can use any berries that are in season or that you have in the freezer. And jars of delicious homemade jelly, with beautifully decorated labels, make nice gifts for your friends and family. So start saving up those old glass jars so you have plenty of containers to fill.

**SKILL LEVEL** ❄ ❄ ❄

**TIME NEEDED** 2 days

**1** Put the saucers in the freezer to chill—these will be used to test the setting point of the jelly.

**2** Cut the lemons in half and squeeze out the juice using a lemon juicer.

**3** Place the berries, sugar, and lemon juice in a large microwaveable bowl and stir until everything is well mixed.

**4** Place the bowl, uncovered, in the microwave and cook on medium power for 2 minutes.

**5** Remove the bowl from the microwave and stir the mixture with a wooden spoon to make sure the sugar is dissolved. Then cook for 3 more minutes, remove it, and stir again.

## YOU WILL NEED

4 cups (1 kg) mixed berries (blueberries, strawberries, raspberries, blackberries)

3 ⅓ cups (670 g) sugar

4 tablespoons fresh lemon juice (about 2–3 lemons)

A lemon juicer

Two saucers

A large microwaveable bowl

A microwave

A ladle

A wooden spoon

A sharp knife

Glass jars with lids (sterilized)

Labels

## DID YOU KNOW?

Berry colors are due to natural plant pigments localized mainly in berry skins and seeds. Berry pigments are usually antioxidants, and berries have a very high nutrient content, making them a "superfruit."

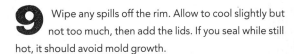

**6** Replace the bowl in the microwave and cook on high power for about 16 minutes, removing it every 3 minutes to give it a stir, or until the jelly reaches its setting point. The mixture will be very hot after heating, so be careful when stirring the mixture.

**7** To check if the jelly is at its setting point, take a teaspoon of the mixture and place it on a chilled saucer from the freezer. Put the saucer back in the freezer for 1 minute. Remove from freezer and run your finger through the jelly. If the mixture wrinkles and a skin forms, then the jelly is ready and at its setting point. If not, continue to cook in the microwave for several minutes more and then retest.

**8** Once it is at its setting point, the jelly can be very carefully ladled into clean jars, which should be warmed first (running them under hot water should do it).

**9** Wipe any spills off the rim. Allow to cool slightly but not too much, then add the lids. If you seal while still hot, it should avoid mold growth.

**10** Don't forget to stick on handwritten labels that tell you what's in the jelly and the year in which you made it. Then you can store it for as long as you like.

**TOP TIP**

If your preserving jars do not have lids, then you can buy ready-made waxed paper tops and lids. The top goes directly onto the jelly, and then the cellophane or material cover is secured on the jar using an elastic band.

# WINTER CHICKEN SOUP

There is nothing more comforting than a bowl of nourishing homemade soup, especially on a cold winter's day. It's just what you need to stay warm and fill you with energy to keep up with your winter adventures. Soup is also very easy to make, using whatever vegetables and ingredients you have in the house, and it is also a great way to use up leftovers. To turn this recipe into a vegetarian option, simply swap the chicken and stock for two tins of canned tomatoes.

| SKILL LEVEL | ❄ |
| TIME NEEDED | 45 minutes |

**1** In a large saucepan, sweat the onion in the oil on a low heat for 5 minutes.

**2** Add the stock, carrots, whole chicken breast, and bay leaf. Season with salt and pepper, and simmer on medium heat until the meat and vegetables are cooked throughly, probably for about 20 minutes.

**3** Remove the chicken breast from the pan and cut it into bite-sized pieces.

**4** Toss half the chicken pieces back into the pan. Using a handheld mixer, blend everything until smooth.

**5** Add the remaining chicken pieces, heat through again, and serve with warm bread.

## YOU WILL NEED

½ onion, peeled and diced

1 tablespoon oil

4 cups (1 liter) chicken stock

3 carrots, peeled and diced

One chicken breast, left whole

Bay leaf

Salt and pepper

### TOP TIP

For a variation on this recipe and a more substantial, chunky soup, do not use a blender, and add a selection of extra vegetables such as leeks, sweetcorn, and potatoes, or pasta shapes.

# WINTER STEW

Stew is a wonderfully warming winter dish. Surprisingly, it takes less than half an hour to actually prepare, and you can then let it simmer for the next two-and-a-half hours, leaving you free to do what you want. This recipe uses beef, but originally Irish stew was made using lamb or mutton. Often, lamb or mutton trimmings were the only basis for the stock. Yet, they still held enough flavors to do justice to this hearty dish.

| | |
|---|---|
| **SKILL LEVEL** | ❄ |
| **TIME NEEDED** | 2–3 hours |

**1** Put flour, salt and pepper, and beef into a large plastic bag. Seal the top, trapping some air in the bag. Then shake to coat the meat evenly in flour.

**2** Heat vegetable oil in the pan over medium-high heat.

**3** Add beef to hot oil and cook, stirring regularly until browned.

**4** Stir in garlic and cook, stirring for about a minute.

**5** Add tomato purée, brown sugar, Worcestershire sauce, thyme, and beef stock.

**6** Bring to a boil, then reduce heat and simmer for one hour.

**7** Add potatoes, onion, and carrots, and stir.

**8** Allow to cook for another hour, until vegetables and meat are tender.

**9** Serve the stew in bowls with crusty bread.

## YOU WILL NEED

3 tablespoons vegetable or sunflower oil

½ cup (60 g) flour

2 ½ cup (450 g) cubed stewing beef

2 cloves garlic, crushed

5 cups (1.2 L) beef stock

2 tablespoons tomato purée

1 tablespoon brown sugar

2 teaspoons thyme

1 tablespoon Worcestershire sauce

6 medium-sized potatoes, peeled and cut into 1-in (2.54-cm) chunks

1 large onion, chopped

4 carrots, peeled and cut into chunks

Salt and pepper, to taste

Large plastic bag

Heavy-based large casserole dish

Metal spoon

# APPLE CRISP

This traditional winter dessert remains popular because it's so delicious and warming. Apples are grown all over the world and are very good for you, as they contain many vitamins and minerals. No wonder the saying goes: "An apple a day keeps the doctor away." Serve this crisp with a dollop of whipped cream or a scoop of ice cream for a truly satisfying dish.

| | |
|---|---|
| SKILL LEVEL | ❄ ❄ |
| TIME NEEDED | 1¼ hour |

**1** Using a small knife, and being extremely careful—you may want to get an adult to help with this bit—peel, core and slice the apples, and put in the bottom of your oven-proof dish.

**2** Sprinkle ¼ cup (50 g) of sugar over apple slices.

**3** After washing your hands, mix and rub the flour, margarine, and remaining sugar together between your fingers until the mixture looks like breadcrumbs.

**4** Stir in the oats and put the mixture on top of the apples.

**5** Put in a preheated oven, 350°F (180°C) for 40–45 minutes.

**6** Serve with ice cream or whipped cream.

## YOU WILL NEED

2 ½ cups (280 g) all-purpose flour

Pinch of salt

¾ cup (170 g) margarine or butter

1 cup (170 g) cane sugar

½ cup (45 g) rolled oats

3 medium cooking apples

Mixing bowl

Small, sharp knife

Apple corer (optional)

Oven-proof dish

## TOP TIP

You can use other fruits such as rhubarb, pears, apricots, and plums—all of which are in season in the winter instead of apples. If you don't have any fresh fruit, you can use canned fruit instead—just drain off some of the juice before adding the topping.

## WARNING

The apples will be scalding hot when the crisp comes out of the oven, so allow the dish to cool slightly before serving, and be careful when eating not to burn your mouth.

# HOMEMADE HOT CHOCOLATE

What could be more comforting and cozy on a cold winter's night than snuggling up with a cup of creamy, homemade hot chocolate? You can use any kind of chocolate for this recipe—you can even use chocolate chips if you have them because they melt easily. For an indulgent treat you can add toppings to your hot chocolate, such as marshmallows, whipped cream, sprinkles, grated chocolate, or chocolate chips.

| SKILL LEVEL | ❄ |
|---|---|
| TIME NEEDED | 20 minutes |

### YOU WILL NEED

⅔ cups (170 g) chopped chocolate

2 cups (500 ml) milk or water

Heat-resistant bowl

A saucepan

A wooden spoon

**1** First, place the chunks of chopped chocolate into a heat-resistant bowl.

**2** Bring a little water to a boil in a saucepan. Turn the heat down to a low boil and place the bowl over the saucepan so that it does not touch the bottom and fits snugly in the rim.

**3** Stir the chocolate occasionally until it has all melted and has a smooth consistency.

**4** Put the melted chocolate to one side while you heat the milk in a saucepan over a low flame. Keep an eye on the chocolate to make sure it doesn't harden.

**5** Add the melted chocolate to the warm milk, mixing well. If you add only a little milk or water to melted chocolate, it forms a solid lump. To make sure that you get a smooth, silky hot chocolate drink rather than a lumpy mess, make sure you follow the recipe to get the right ratio of liquid to chocolate.

**6** Allow to cool slightly before sipping and enjoying your delicious hot chocolate drink.

# CHOCOLATE BROWNIES

This simple-to-follow recipe gives you two dozen perfect chocolate brownies—gooey on the inside, and lovely and crispy on the outside. Serve with a large dollop of your favorite ice cream and enjoy. If kept in an airtight container, you should be able to keep the brownies fresh for up to four days. If you don't trust yourself not to eat them all right away, you can always put some in the freezer for a later date.

| | |
|---|---|
| **SKILL LEVEL** | ❄ ❄ |
| **TIME NEEDED** | 1 hour |

**1** Preheat the oven to 350°F (180°C). Grease the pan and line the base with greaseproof paper.

**2** Break up the dark chocolate into pieces and place in a microwaveable bowl.

**3** Heat in a microwave on medium power for 10 to 15 seconds, and then check the consistency. Keep reheating for 10 to 15 seconds until the chocolate is smooth and fully melted. Set aside to cool slightly.

**4** Put the butter and sugar into a bowl and beat with electric mixer until light and fluffy.

**5** Gradually add the beaten eggs, mixing well after each.

**6** Beat in vanilla extract, then pour the cooled, melted

## YOU WILL NEED

6 in (15 cm) square baking pan

Greaseproof paper

2¼ cup (200 g) dark chocolate

A microwaveable bowl

A microwave

Wooden and metal spoons

½ cup (100 g) unsalted butter, softened

1 ⅓ cup (250 g) granulated sugar

A mixing bowl

An electric mixer

4 large eggs, beaten

1 teaspoon vanilla extract

⅔ cup (60 g) all-purpose flour

⅔ cup (60 g) cocoa powder

A sifter

## TOP TIPS

Should your chocolate brownies become a bit stale, just give them a 10-second blast in the microwave and serve warm with ice cream. That should freshen them up again.

Be patient when melting chocolate in the microwave. If you zap it too quickly, you may burn it.

chocolate into the mixture and mix thoroughly.

**7** Sift the flour and cocoa powder into the mixture, and gently fold in using a metal spoon.

**8** When fully combined, spoon the mixture into the prepared pan and spread evenly.

**9** Bake in the oven for about 20–25 minutes until firm to the touch. It should still be soft in the middle, but the top should be cracked. (The chocolate will continue to cook for a short while after it comes out of the oven.)

**10** Allow to cool for at least 20 minutes in the pan and then remove the brownie and place it on a cutting board, then cut into pieces.

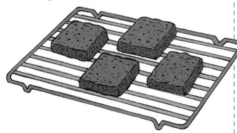

# CLUB SANDWICH

The great thing about making a club sandwich for lunch is that, although it tastes mouth-wateringly delicious, it's actually quite good for you.

| | |
|---|---|
| **SKILL LEVEL** | ❄ |
| **TIME NEEDED** | 1 hour |

## YOU WILL NEED

**2 slices of bread**

**Butter or margarine**

**A knife**

**Toothpicks**

**Fillings of your choice (such as turkey, ham, cheese, tomatoes, cucumber, etc.)**

**1** Spread both slices of bread with butter or margarine. Then cut the slices in half.

**2** Spread three of the halves with the toppings of your choice—for example, mustard, ham, and cheese on one, and perhaps mayonnnaise, chicken, and lettuce on another, and so on.

**3** Stack the three layers on top of each other and top them off with the fourth slice.

**4** Carefully cut in half and hold each stack together with a toothpick.

# PLUM PIE

Pie is a favorite all year round, and is easy to adjust to suit whatever fruit is currently in season. Certain varieties of plums are still in season in October and early November, when many fresh fruits have ceased to grow, which makes this plum pie a good option for fall and winter.

| SKILL LEVEL | ❄ ❄ |
|---|---|
| TIME NEEDED | 3 hours |

**1** Preheat the oven to 400°F (200°C). Place the baking sheet in the oven to heat up.

**2** Thickly slice plums and place in a saucepan with sugar and ground cloves, if using.

**3** Heat and simmer until the sugar dissolves and the plums are soft and juicy.

**4** Put the cornstarch in a cup and spoon on some of the juice from the plums to mix it into a smooth consistency.

**5** Pour the cornstarch mix into the cooking fruit and mix well. Boil for a few minutes, stirring constantly until the mixture has thickened. Remove from heat.

**6** Now roll out two-thirds of the pastry on a clean, floured surface. Use to carefully line pie dish, allowing the pastry to hang over the edges a little. Press the pastry down gently into the tin.

## YOU WILL NEED

### FOR THE PIE CRUST:

1 lb (500 g) pack shortcrust pastry

Flour (for dusting)

1 egg, beaten, to glaze

### FOR THE FILLING:

4 cups (900 g) plums, with pits removed

1 1/2 cups (140 g) brown sugar (plus a little extra for decorating)

1/2 teaspoon ground cloves (optional)

1 heaping tablespoon of cornstarch

### EQUIPMENT:

A large saucepan

A rolling pin

9-inch (23-cm) pie dish

A large baking sheet

A pastry brush

Wooden and metal spoons

**7** Pour the plum mixture into the pie. Roll out the remaining pastry until it is slightly larger than the pie dish.

**8** Drape the pastry lid over the plum filling, pinching the edges together well. Using a sharp knife, cut a small cross in the middle of the pastry lid.

**9** Now brush the pastry top evenly with the beaten egg and sprinkle with extra sugar.

**10** Using oven mitts, place the dish on the hot baking sheet. Bake for 25–30 minutes, until golden brown.

**11** Serve your pie hot or cold, and either on its own or with a scoop of ice cream, whipped cream, or custard, using the recipe below.

## HOMEMADE CUSTARD

If you're feeling really ambitious, you can make your own custard to accompany your plum pie. It takes a little patience, but the results are well worth the effort.

**1** In a large bowl, beat the egg yolks with the sugar.

**2** Heat the milk and allow to almost come to a boil.

**3** Pour the hot milk over the egg yolks, whisking hard. When completely mixed in, return to the pan.

**4** Stir over low heat until the mixture thickens enough to coat the back of a spoon. This will take about 5–6 minutes.

**5** Remove from the heat and add the vanilla extract. Serve with your plum pie immediately.

**YOU WILL NEED**

A large mixing bowl

A wooden spoon

2 egg yolks

1 tablespoon granulated sugar

1¼ cups (290 ml) milk

A saucepan

A metal whisk

1 teaspoon vanilla extract

# CRISPY CEREAL CAKES

This is one of the easiest recipes you could ever want to make —there isn't even any cooking involved—yet the result is a satisfying treat that can be enjoyed at any time of day. These crispy cakes are delicious just as they are, but if you want something different, you can add raisins, or decorate each one with brightly colored candies or candied cherries. This recipe will make 12 to 14 cups.

| SKILL LEVEL | ❄ |
| --- | --- |
| TIME NEEDED | 2 hours |

**1** Break the chocolate into small chunks and place in a microwaveable bowl.

**2** Microwave on medium heat in short bursts of 10–15 seconds, stirring between each session, until melted.

**3** Add the butter, chopped into small pieces so that it melts faster, and stir until melted.

**4** Add the syrup, and stir thoroughly until the ingredients are well combined.

**5** Add the crispy cereal and stir into the chocolate mixture until well coated.

**6** Leave the chocolate rice mixture to cool for a few minutes and then spoon it into the muffin cups.

**7** If adding decorations, press on while the chocolate is still soft.

**8** Leave to cool completely before eating.

## YOU WILL NEED

1 cup (100 g) milk or dark chocolate

A microwaveable bowl

A metal spoon

$^1/_4$ cup (60 g) unsalted butter

3 tablespoons light corn syrup

$4^1/_4$ cups (90 g) cripsy rice cereal

Paper muffin cups

### TOP TIP

Instead of using a microwave to melt the chocolate, you could melt it in a bowl placed over a saucepan of simmering water.

# OAT BARS

Delicious and nutritious, these tasty bars are the perfect accompaniment for activity-filled winter days. Another name for them is Hudson Bay Bread, and they have their origins in scout expeditions in Canada. With this recipe, you can make the perfect oat bars for filling you up when you're in need of an energy boost.

| | |
|---|---|
| **SKILL LEVEL** | ❄ ❄ |
| **TIME NEEDED** | 1 hour |

**1** Preheat the oven to 375°F (190°C).

**2** Melt the butter in a small saucepan, making sure you don't let it turn brown.

**3** Using sunflower oil, grease the baking tin.

**4** Mix the oats, dried fruit (if you are using them), and syrup in a mixing bowl.

**5** Add the sugar and the melted butter. Mix well with a wooden spoon.

**6** Tip the mixture into the prepared baking pan and press it down flat with the back of the wooden spoon.

**7** Using oven mitts, put the pan in the oven and bake for 25–30 minutes until golden and turning brown at the edges.

**8** Carefully remove the pan from the oven wearing oven mitts.

**9** Cut into 16 slices and leave to cool in the pan.

**10** When completely cool, remove from the pan and enjoy!

## YOU WILL NEED

²/₃ cup (150 g) butter

A small saucepan

1 tablespoon sunflower oil, for greasing

A shallow baking pan, 12 x 10 in (30 x 25 cm)

2 ¼ cups (200 g) rolled oats

¹/₂ cup (70 g) raisins or chopped dried apricots (optional)

2 tablespoons light corn syrup

A mixing bowl

1 cup (100 g) cane sugar

A wooden spoon

## TOP TIP

Oat bars are ideal snacks for when you are hiking on the trail because they release energy slowly.

# PERFECT PANCAKES

In France, they're called crêpes; in America, they're eaten for breakfast; and in Britain, they're consumed in large quantities with sugar and lemon on one specific day of the year. What are we talking about? Pancakes, of course!

| | |
|---|---|
| **SKILL LEVEL** | ✳ |
| **TIME NEEDED** | 45 minutes |

**1** In a large bowl, whisk the egg into the milk. Put the flour and salt in a mixing bowl, and gradually add the milk and egg mixture, stirring vigorously all the time to remove lumps. The finished batter should be runny and have the consistency of cream.

**2** Add a drop of oil to the pan and heat until hot on a high heat. Add two large spoonfuls of batter and tilt the pan until it is thinly but evenly coated.

**3** The first side only takes about 1 minute to cook. When it's done, flip the pancake. Cook the other side and then place on a plate, add the toppings of your choice, roll, and enjoy!

**4** If you're feeling confident, you can toss the pancake rather than just flipping it with a spatula. Shake the pan to make sure the cooked side isn't sticking to it, then swing the pan forward with a flick of the wrist. The pancake should jump out of the pan, neatly turn over, and land cooked-side-up. You might want to practice that a few times!

## YOU WILL NEED

A large bowl

1 egg

1¼ cups (280 ml) of milk

8 heaping teaspoons of all-purpose flour

A pinch of salt

A mixing bowl

1 tablespoon of light oil such as vegetable or sunflower oil

A heavy-based frying pan

Toppings of your choice

## DID YOU KNOW?

The world's biggest pancake was cooked in Rochdale, Greater Manchester, England, in 1994. It was 50 feet (15 meters) in diameter, weighed 3 metric tons, and had an estimated two million calories.

# CHOCOLATE LOG

A homemade chocolate roll dusted with icing sugar is the perfect centerpiece for a special occasion. It's a challenge to make, but once you get the hang of it, the results are well worth the effort—and if you follow these simple instructions you should have no problems. The tricky part is rolling up the cooked cake without it breaking, so be extra careful when doing that step. And remember, any minor cracks and breaks can be disguised with the icing, so don't get disheartened if it doesn't go perfectly, especially the first time.

**1** Preheat the oven to 350°F (180°C) and grease the Swiss roll tin. Then line the tin with greaseproof paper.

**2** Sift the flour and cocoa powder together.

**3** Using an electric mixer, beat the egg whites until they are stiff, and then gradually add the granulated sugar, beating continuously until the mixture is thick and the sugar is completely dissolved.

**4** Beat in the egg yolks and add the hot water.

**5** Using a metal spoon, fold in the sifted flour and cocoa.

**6** Pour the mixture into the Swiss roll tin and bake in the oven for 12–15 minutes.

**SKILL LEVEL** ❄ ❄ ❄

**TIME NEEDED** 1 hour

## YOU WILL NEED

Swiss roll tin

Greaseproof paper

1 ¼ cups (125 g) all-purpose flour

2 tablespoons cocoa powder

A sifter

A mixing bowl

An electric mixer

3 large eggs, separated

⅔ cups (125 g) granulated sugar

2 tablespoons hot water

Wooden and metal spoons

Sifted icing sugar

Extra granulated sugar for rolling

## FOR THE FILLING:

⅔ cup (140 g) butter, softened

2 ¼ cups (280 g) icing sugar

1–2 drops vanilla extract

1–2 tablespoons milk

### DID YOU KNOW?

Bûche de Noël is the French name for a chocolate log, which is served at Christmas time. Traditionally, Bûche de Noël is decorated with icing sugar to resemble snow on a Yule log, and the tradition has stuck so that chocolate logs are usually dusted with icing sugar when served at any time of year.